Good Grief: A Journey

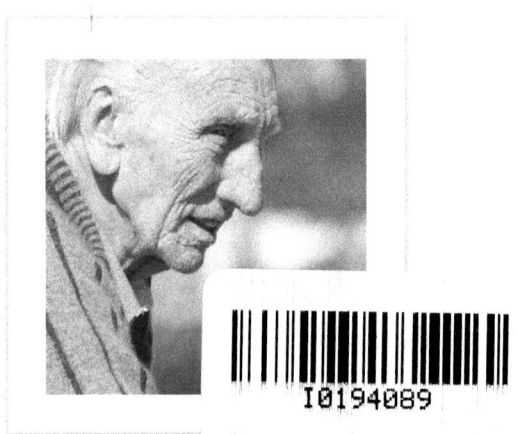

Kevin Warner

Copyright © 2019 by Kevin Warner
All rights reserved. This book or any
portion thereof may not be reproduced
or used in any manner whatsoever
without the express written permission
of the publisher except for the use of brief
quotations in a book review.

Notice
To the fullest extent of the law, neither the
Publisher nor the author assume any liability
for any injury and/or damage to persons or
property as a matter of products liability,
negligence or otherwise, or from any use
or operation of any methods, products,
instructions or ideas contained in the material
herein.

First Published by www.lulu.com in 2019

ISBN: 978-0-244-82163-0

"I will not say: do not weep; for not all tears are an evil." J.R.R. Tolkien

"Because I could not stop for Death, he kindly stopped for me." Emily Dickinson

Contents

Acknowledgements 5
1 – The Move 6
2 – The Decline 17
3 – A Decision is Made 30
4 – The Return 34
5 – Homecoming 40
6 – Caravanning 46
7 – The Calm Before the Storm 51
8 – It Hits the Fan 61
9 – Derriford Hospital 68
10 – On the Ward 73
11 – Coming Home 84
12 – Changes 97
13 – The Impossible Question 109
14 – Decline 115
15 – Carers 124
16 – Life in the New Flat 128
17 – The End is Nigh 140
18 – The End 148
19 – The Aftermath 155
20 – Life after Death 162
21 – A Final Word 167

Acknowledgements

I'd like to thank the doctors at the Friary House Surgery. Without their care and high level of professionalism much of the support I needed would never have been found. I'd also like to thank the staff of St Luke's Hospice in Plymouth. Their palliative care nursing and social care teams provided dad, and me, with such warm care.

1 – The Move

Back in November 2003 I had just finished working on a major project, it had been full on pressure with strict deadlines. The project had been stressful and exhausting for twelve months, involving travelling all over the UK, staying in budget hotels, working into the early hours and getting up at 5am… I was ready for a break. Spain beaconed. I had always loved Spain. My very first family holiday abroad had been to Spain, in the north-eastern town of Salou on the Costa Daurada, in the Tarragona province. That was back in 1976. All I remember is the sun, sea, sand, food (which had been terrible in the hotel but wonderful in the little restaurant we found) and a day trip we had to Barcelona, about an hour and a half coach drive east. During that day trip we toured the city and, although I was very young, I loved the place. It was shocking and breathtakingly beautiful all at once.

After a year of full-on stress, I felt the need of a dose of Spanish sun and three weeks in Barcelona was just the thing to recharge the batteries, Barcelona, even in winter, is a wonderful city.

I visited the sights, ate delicious food, drank a little too much, and spent lots of time resting, relaxing and thinking. I got into a routine, waking around 10am and walking to a little café for breakfast and coffee. After breakfast I'd walk for a while in Park Güell and ponder the fantastical Gaudí architecture and read for a few hours. Sometime after 2pm I'd grab lunch and head back to the hotel for an afternoon siesta. During the evening I'd find a little bar, have a few drinks, get dinner and round the day off with a few more drinks, enjoying the Spanish atmosphere until late.

It was an enjoyable holiday, the weather was sunny and warm, well, warm for November. I think out of the three weeks it rained on just two days, two days I couldn't read in the park but there were plenty of beautiful cafés to sit and read in. The best thing about the holiday was the time it allowed to think.

I got to thinking about how much I wanted a change, a new start in a new country. I considered moving to Spain, I love Spain and the Spanish culture, but I wanted a new start in an English speaking country, partly because I wanted to get up and running in a new country from the start but mostly because I was lazy and didn't want to have to learn a new language while learning to live in a new country.

My father was born in Australia. His parents moved to Western Australia in around 1925 as part of a post WWI resettlement scheme, similar to the more famous 'ten-pound poms' scheme from the 1940's. The trip was not a success, the family lost a child, the land was almost unworkable and the isolation was intolerable.

The catalogue of disasters actually started before my grandparents made the move. Shortly before they were due to set out for Australia the family received a telegram from family members already living in Northcliffe, the settlement they were relocating to. The telegram simply said: "cancel all arrangements, hand off." Words cost money, so brevity was the key. However, in this case a few more words may have been helpful, as my grandparents didn't understand... hand off what? They didn't have any way to contact the family already in Northcliffe, so they continued with the trip. When they arrived in Australia, they discovered that my grandfather's brother had been working to cut down the gigantic Karri trees on their land, using dynamite. He had misjudged the job and blown his own hand off. They had been planning to return to the UK so contacted my grandparents to warn them not to make the journey.

My father was born in 1931 and in 1932 the family made the move back to England... but Australia was not finished punishing the family. On the sea voyage back to England my grandfather was lost overboard! During the voyage my grandfather suffered a breakdown and had been confined to a cabin. Violet, my dad's older sister, took her dad his midday meal, only to find the cabin empty. A search of the ship found no sign of him. So, it was assumed he'd escaped the cabin and either slipped or jumped overboard. Although my dad believed that he was thrown overboard by members of the ship's crew, because he was causing so much trouble.

Considering all the pain, heartache and horror of their Australian adventure I, for some reason, still decided to try my own Australian move.

A quick bit of research found the requirements for living and working in Australia and, to my relief, found I was eligible for a visa but talking to someone, at the Australian High Commission in London, I discovered I was also able to apply for Australian citizenship through descent. I just had to get a certified copy of my father's birth certificate from Western Australia; my father had altered his original birth certificate so he could join the merchant navy two years before he was really old enough. It was easy, a few emails later I was corresponding to the right person in a town called Pemberton, the town nearest to the Settlement my father was born in. By June 2004 I was an Australian citizen before ever setting foot on Australian soil, I had a beautiful certificate and Australian passport to prove it. I had also found a job in Australia, although that wouldn't start until January 2005. So, I booked a one-way flight, and hotel, and suddenly found myself in Perth, Australia.

I quickly found a rental property, to give me a base, and even started a temporary job until January. Those first few months were hectic and exciting. I was busy looking for a home and learning all the little differences between the UK and Australia. I got a WA driver's license, a Medicare card, a tax file number and bank account. I was busy acclimatising to my new environment, so it was probably the worst time for my family to decide to visit… but that's when they did choose to come and stay. My father came over with my aunt and uncle. They arrived the day before my birthday in November and stayed for a month. Their visit was useful in some respects, I drove them around to various places of interest, including Northcliffe, my father's birthplace. In other respects their visit was a complete pain in the proverbial, while I was getting ready to start an important new job I had to play tour guide, I enjoyed their visit but thought they could have visited at a better time.

They went home at the start of December and left me to my first Australian Christmas, I spent that Christmas Day having the traditional Aussie Christmas BBQ, it was strange having Christmas in 40°C heat... something I never quite got used too. After Christmas came New Year, which again was celebrated with a BBQ, the BBQ is a big thing in Aussie culture. Then came January, and another BBQ on the 26th (Australia Day), and I started my new job and life settled into a wonderful routine. A routine that was to be shattered in mid 2008.

In March 2008 my dad rang and, after the usual pleasantries, said he had decided to move to Australia and live out his retirement in the sun – I remember the day clearly, the rain was hammering down and later that night the wind would rip the roof off my garage! It was good news, moving to the other side of the world, to make a new start, was exciting but, not having any family or friends, I felt very isolated. It would be good having my dad living near.

A month or so went by, with regular phone calls, and finally the day came when I had to drive to Perth International Airport to pick him up. I had chosen to settle in rural Western Australia, a place called Capel, roughly 132 miles south of Perth. His plane was due to land at 11:30pm, so after work I went home and got changed and had a leisurely drive to the airport. Typical for my dad, his flight was delayed but only by about 15 minutes, although he seemed to take an eternity getting through passport control. He had flown out using his UK passport, he didn't have an Australian one yet, but no return ticket. It took immigration sometime to verify his citizenship status but after a two hour wait he was finally cleared and we went off to find the car.

He slept for most of the drive back to the house but was fully awake when we pulled into the driveway. Whenever he got home he always liked a cup of tea, even if he had just popped out for a few minutes, even if the reason for going out was to have a coffee. So, we had a cup of tea, which was not up to his exacting standards, and a long chat. He was going to stay with me until he found a place of his own. That was ok, the house was big, Australian homes tend to be bigger than homes in England. Land, especially in rural areas, was much less expensive. So, there was plenty of space for the both of us. After a few weeks it was obvious that he had stopped looking for his own place and I had stopped asking how the search was going.

Many people likened the two of us to the tv show 'Fraser', without the dog. For a long time it worked out well, we may have lived in the same house but we had our separate lives. I had work, trips away, for work and pleasure, friends and the usual impedimenta of a life; and so did he. We also did things together, a few trips around Australia, a couple of cruises, lots of day trips, often to vineyards, and countless shopping expeditions.

It worked well, it was actually good to have him close, when he moved to Australia he was a fit and vital 77 year old. He worked out in the garden, doing in one day what would have taken me a week, did some decorating and went out everyday for walks. Slowly, however, his health deteriorated.

Dad had smoked almost all his life, he grew up during the War and his eldest sister, Alma, met, and fell in love with, an American GI. To curry favour with his new 'family' Vin, the GI in question, would bring things home from the American base, things that were hard to get for ordinary Limeys like us: stockings, chocolate and cigarettes. As a 12-year-old boy, dad was not that interested in the stockings, except for their comedy value, he liked the chocolate but he got hooked on the cigarettes. From then on he was a smoker and smoked for the vast majority of the rest of his life.

He did briefly give up smoking in 1982, he and my sister-in-law, Kath, visited a hypnotherapist to quit smoking. The therapy was spread over three sessions, dad and Kath went together, although they had separate appointments. After the third session it appeared to have work, they both gave up. Kath never smoked again. Dad also gave up, we didn't see him smoke… until he was spotted smoking in secret, in his bedroom. He maintains that he did give up for a couple of weeks but…!

So, he had been a smoker for sixty odd years and that was about to catch up with him. Sixty years of smoking unfiltered, hand rolled, cigarettes is going to do damage in some form, for dad that damage was going to manifest itself in the form of Chronic Obstructive Pulmonary Disease (COPD), a degenerative condition that hugely impacts mobility and quality of life.

2 – The Decline

My father had always been very active, although he did have his health issues. Over his life he had had a number of jobs, all of them hard. His first job had been at a power station, he described this job as a cleaner. What he really did was to climb into parts of the station that funnelled noxious by-products out of the station and chip away the accumulated detritus. A dirty, hard and dangerous job. Although hearing him talk about his time at the power station, that was the least of his worries.

One lunchtime, in the worker's ready room, his foreman asked a young, and naïve, dad to watch the eggs he was boiling for lunch; do not, under any circumstances, let them boil for longer than three minutes! Dad, being a typical teenage boy, got distracted and the eggs were left for more than ten minutes. When the foreman came back to the ready room, he threw the eggs at dad and, from that moment on, gave dad the worst jobs possible. So, he then ran away to sea.

He started working at the power station when he was 14 but by the age of 15 he had joined the merchant navy. That's why I had to write off to Australia for a copy of his birth certificate for my application for Aussie citizenship, he had scratched out his year of birth so he could pass for 18. He became a general dogs body, his description, on an ocean liner, the RMS Otranto, doing everything from running messages between officers to serving passengers in the restaurant.

He visited Africa, America and Australia, but he wasn't happy, he missed home and his mates, and he didn't enjoy having to be polite to rude people. When he got back to good old Blighty he left the ship for good.

After the merchant navy he bounced aimlessly from job to job until he was called up for national service, he served in the Army in Egypt, during the build-up to the Suez Crisis. His time in the Army was both his best of times and his worst of times. He joined the Royal Signals, as a motorbike dispatch rider, and became a 'white helmet' rider. It was a dangerous job, he saw a number of his fellow riders killed in attacks against the British military. His bike, and all military vehicles, was fitted with a pole with a blade at the front, so any wires strung across the road would be cut before the rider was beheaded, something that had happened a few times.

There was a lot about this time he never spoke of but one thing he was very proud of was his driving test. He was sent, with a bunch of raw recruits for driver instruction, after a couple of hours instruction they were all passed. He had a driver's license, which allowed him to ride his motorbike and almost any other military car, jeep or truck. It was also valid in civilian life too. He liked to boast that he'd never sat a driver's test, although this wasn't exactly true. He loved riding a motorbike and enjoyed driving, so when his national service was finished he trained as a bus driver, he didn't enjoy that, and then became a lorry driver. His army driving license allowed him to drive heavy goods vehicles but not passenger vehicles, so he had to pass his bus driver's test. For the rest of his working life he continued driving lorries, he was a long-distance tanker driver, carrying hazardous liquids.

He was a tall man with a job that required long periods of sitting and short periods of frenetic activity, climbing up and down on his tanker and hauling heavy hoses around. It's no wonder he suffered with severe back pain. In the 1970s he spent several weeks in hospital on traction because of a slipped disk. Back pain was his constant companion, together with sciatic nerve pain. As a child I watched him hobble, in agony, to work. To this day I don't know how he did it. In my mid-thirties I suffered a sciatic nerve attack, it floored me, I'd never experienced such pain and I was off work for nearly a month… and my job could be done sitting down. Dad used to battle on, doing a hard, physical, job, through the pain.

His job also exposed him to harmful chemicals, and this was at a time health & safety was in its infancy. Throughout his life, from a young child to old age, he suffered a number of battles with pneumonia. This, plus the damage caused by inhaling years of harsh chemicals and decades of smoking, weakened his lungs. We noticed he was having breathing problems when he was about 79 years old, to start with he put it down to 'getting old' but I had my concerns. His GP sent him to a respiratory consultant who diagnosed COPD, an umbrella term that includes emphysema, which is what he had.

His decline was steady and progressive. At the time of his diagnosis he was able to walk about freely, drive, and generally potter about the house and garden, apart from getting 'winded' while walking strenuously he was able to do all the things he usually did. At about this time my brother visited from the UK.

We did the usual touristy things, visiting many tourist attractions and places of interest and dad came along. He would walk for miles. The only concession to his illness was regular stops to catch his breath, this was often masked as 'photo op' breaks.

In 2011 I took dad on a cruise around New Zealand, although he hadn't enjoyed his time in the merchant navy he had always loved boats and being on the water. The cruise started in Sydney, crossed the Tasman Sea, went anticlockwise around New Zealand and finally back to Sydney. He loved the trips across the Tasman Sea but the trips ashore were getting difficult. By this time he found walking much more difficult, having to stop for a rest every 50 metres or so. He tried to walk but it was a struggle, but he did enjoy the time on the boat.

The following year I organised a cruise from Singapore to Sydney. Again, he enjoyed the time on the boat, but he was really struggling with walking. Then, early in the cruise, his health deteriorated so much I had to call in the ship's doctor, who diagnosed pneumonia. We were approaching Darwin and he was so ill the doctor seriously considered airlifting him ashore. In the end it was decided he could rest in his cabin until we arrived at Darwin and waiting on the harbourside, on our arrival in port, was an ambulance to rush him to hospital. There he had a chest x-ray and was hooked up to some powerful antibiotics via an IV drip.

The medical staff at the hospital confirmed the ship's doctor's diagnosis and debated whether he should re-join the cruise or should he stay in hospital. They finally agreed to allow him to leave and re-join the ship. He was extremely weak and unable to do anything more than get to his balcony and watch the world go by. In those days he looked so diminished and weak, it was a sad preview of what was to come.

When the ship finally arrived in Sydney dad was still so very weak. He could walk just a few steps before having to rest but we eventually got off the ship and to the hotel, it was lucky I had booked a couple of nights in a hotel before our flight back to Perth. As well as the physical symptoms dad was feeling so very depressed. He was terrified about what was happening to him, and of the future, but most of all he was worried about being a burden to me. I tried to reassure him that he could never be a burden and that whatever the future was we would face it together, no matter what I said he was scared. It was the first time I had seen him like this.

All my life my dad had been a strong and active man, as a child, as most children do, I thought he could do anything. Apart from his afternoon nap, which was a daily ritual never to be missed, he was active, always doing something. He had never been beaten by circumstance, he had always bounced back and come out fighting. Now, he was a shadow of the man I knew and it was breaking my heart.

We stayed in the Sydney hotel for two days, three nights. In ordinary times it would have been a lovely place to stay, in an area known as The Rocks. The view from my hotel window was dominated by the Opera House and the hotel itself was luxurious, great food in the restaurant and friendly, helpful, staff. The only negative about the hotel was the bar closed at 9pm! It was a lovely hotel in one of the most attractive parts of one of the most exciting cities in the world but none of that mattered.

The flight back to Perth was horrendous. Dad's COPD combined with the pneumonia and the aircraft's air filtration system, made it a hellish nightmare for him but we made it back. It was late at night when we got to Perth airport and I asked dad if he wanted to get a hotel but he just wanted to get home, a three hour drive away. I understood his desire to get home so I left him at the airport and went in search of the car.

Leaving Perth at the start of the, so called, holiday we left from Perth International but returned to the domestic airport, not just separate terminals but separate airports. I found the car, and for a scary moment it wouldn't start, and got back to the airport, to find dad surrounded by people, I was terrified something had happened to him but no, a group of travellers had started talking to him and stayed with him out of concern… a brief moment of human kindness that renewed my belief in the goodness of people, we don't have enough of those.

The drive back to the house was uneventful, he managed to sleep through the entire drive, even my near miss with a mob of kangaroos. Apart from the close encounter with Skippy, the drive was good, we made excellent time and arrived home. Dad managed to get in doors and to bed, where he stayed for a few days. I called the doctor the following day and later that day the GP came out to the house. He agreed with the diagnosis of the ship's doctor, and the doctors at the Darwin Hospital, prescribed some more antibiotics and said he'd make another appointment for the consultant.

After a few weeks dad recovered a little but he was weakened by the battle with pneumonia, dad said it was his eighth time having pneumonia, the first time was as a six or seven year old child growing up in the Eastend of London. Even after his recovery he was limited in what he could do. He could still dress and wash himself, although it took a long time, and he managed to walk around the house and get out into the garden, but he couldn't walk to the post-box. He was able to drive and would go for a drive to the local shops, although he couldn't do much more than buy a paper or go into the bank. He felt ashamed that I had to do the main shopping, cleaning, cooking, washing, gardening and everything else. He felt useless, even when I said that it wasn't a problem, and it really wasn't, he was so proud and independent that he hated not being able to do things for himself.

Then his brother died. Cliff was a couple of years older than dad, and also born in Australia. Growing up during the Second World War had been tough, they had been evacuated together, first to Hastings, which had been a fantastic time. They were given into the care of a pair of eccentric and wealthy sisters. The boys were picked up at the station by a chauffeur in a Rolls-Royce, and were totally spoiled for their stay, which was sadly too short, one of the sisters became ill and died and the surviving sister couldn't continue caring for the boys, so they returned to London. Then they were evacuated, again, to a farm in Wales, which was a nightmare for dad. Cliff was that much older than dad, so he was able to work on the farm, dad was smaller and couldn't do the same work, and the farmer would always get very angry with him. The conditions in the farmhouse were not great either.

They used to tell the story of when their mother went to Wales to visit her boys. So horrified was she at the conditions the boys were living in that she took them back to London. Apparently, it was so bad that London during the Blitz was preferable to Narbeth. Dad described it as slavery. He had always been close to Cliff and news of his death was devastating. Just a few months later his sister, Violet, died.

Violet had been the only surviving member of the family to actually remember life in Australia back then, she was twelve years older than dad. She remembered walking five miles, barefoot, to a ramshackle, single room, schoolhouse. She remembered the relentless and exhausting work of clearing (or trying to clear) the forest. She remembered the death of their brother Charles, who for some reason has always been referred to as Waggy. And she remembered the utter misery of life in the Northcliffe Settlement. When the family decided to return to the UK, Violet became a second parent to Alma, dad and Cliff, their father having disappeared during the voyage home, believed lost overboard. Losing two of his siblings so close together brought it home just how far away from his family he was.

3 – A Decision is Made

After the deaths of his brother and sister, and his increasing ill health, dad was getting progressively more depressed. He was finding it more difficult to simply get out of bed. He had always been regular in his habits, he had a routine and he stuck to it, no matter whether he was home or on holiday. Get up, drink three cups of tea (and smoke three cigarettes, when he still smoked), perform his ablutions and have breakfast. The whole process usually took an hour and a half, and it didn't matter where he was, the routine never altered. It was still the same but just a tad later than it had been.

He would wake up at about 6am, struggle to go from a lying position to sitting on the edge of the bed and then sit and rest. Then struggle to put his slippers and dressing gown on. The process of getting up took half an hour. And he refused to accept any help, this was private, for him only. It didn't matter that I not only was able to help him but was very willing to help. He wanted to be independent, he had already given up much of his autonomy and was not willing to yield this. This far and no more.

Once up he spent his days sitting watching tv or dozing in the chair. He often said he liked to get up early so he could have a good nap in the chair before elevenses. At this point he was still able to make his own cups of tea and a sandwich for lunch, although I had some washing up to do when I got home from work.

When I got home he would always put the kettle on and we'd have a cuppa together. I would invariably have some work to do, so after the tea I'd disappear into my home office and he'd watch some tv quiz show, usually Millionaire Hotseat (he loved to hate the presenter, Eddie McGuire). I'd then come back into the house and start cooking, we had an open plan living space with the kitchen, family room area and dining area all in one. Which meant while cooking I was with him, so we'd discuss things, everything about my day at work, what I was cooking and him asking me questions from the quiz show; he liked to test my general knowledge like that!

We'd eat together, while watching the news and Egg Heads. After I'd washed up he would watch a couple of movies and I'd disappear into my lounge to listen to music and read. At the weekends we would often go for a drive, not far though. He liked to get out of the house but didn't like to go too far. That was his life, and mine.

We often talked, after Cliff and Violet died he would talk about the old days, what it was like to grow up poor in the Eastend. He'd talk about some of the scrapes he'd gotten into, their holidays hopping in Kent, and how much he missed the family. Slowly the discussions got around to the possibility of returning to the UK.

In 2014 I was told that I would be able to take long service leave in 2015. This is a wonderful part of Aussie culture, most organisations, big and small, offer their employees long service leave after between eight and ten years of continuous service. You then have a choice how to use your long service. You can take it all at once as six months off at full pay or a year at half pay, or you can break it up to use it as extra holiday time over the coming years. Some people even 'sell' it back to their employer.

Knowing that I had long service leave coming up it was a good opportunity to go back to the UK. I could take six months, full pay, to take dad back, stay with him until he got settled in and decide whether I would stay in the UK or return to Australia. Dad liked the idea, so we made the arrangements, renewing passports and so on.

4 – The Return

We lived in a rural community, south of Perth in Western Australia. Between two holiday destinations, the 'Ocean' city of Bunbury and the surfing centre of Busselton. It was a lovely place to live, quiet and tranquil. I'd wake up to kangaroos roaming the garden. However, living in Australia is not the paradise dream many people think it is. Much of the wildlife is out to do you significant harm, the weather, in one way or another, wants to kill you, and quite a bit of the land itself is deadly… whether it be from killing you by thirst, heat, bushfire or flooding. Strangely enough, you get used to all that and life goes on. Our little house had become a home, we enjoyed the garden, and the lifestyle allowed plenty of time for recreation and relaxation.

It was a tough decision to come back to the UK, that shows just how much dad missed his remaining family, especially his eldest son and his grandson. So, after passports were renewed, it was time to book flights and organise accommodation for our arrival back in England.

I always used a local travel agent, yes everything could be done online myself but a proper travel agent is much easier, just tell them what you want and let them do everything. Chances are they will find better value flights and accommodation which will more than pay for any agency fees. I walked into the agency one evening after work. That was when the first problem barred our way. The agent found that every airline she tried required dad to undergo a medical and provide them with a letter saying he was fit for travel.

His GP wasn't happy doing that so another appointment with the consultant had to be made. Now, in the UK we are very privileged, we have the wonderful NHS which, with all its faults, is still the best universal health care system in the world. In Australia they have Medicare, a form of medical subsidy. At point of delivery the medical care must be paid for and then a portion of that cost is claimed back through Medicare. A typical visit to a GP can cost $100 (about £45) and then Medicare will reimburse you $65. An x-ray, CT-scan, MRI or similar can cost up to $2000 at point of service. A visit to a consultant maybe $200. Don't even think about calling for an ambulance, they are not covered by Medicare and cost around $1000.

So, apart from the running around there was the expense of simply getting a doctor to say dad could fly home. There were some caveats about flying. Dad's breathing had become significantly worse, so the consultant was concerned about being in an aircraft cabin for such a long time, but finally conceded that it would be alright. Then there was the logistics of getting to and through the airport. Dad couldn't walk far, after just a few steps he found he was so out of breath that he'd have to stop and rest. He hated the idea of a wheelchair so resisted it, but the doctor suggested it would make the journey much easier, so we agreed. I had been talking about one for a long time, but it needed a consultant to convince him.

All that took about six weeks, but I was finally able to go back to the travel agent, medical letter in hand, to book flights. After a lengthy discussion about us not needing a visa, the flights were booked, a hotel near

Heathrow was booked and everything was organised. We had ten weeks until the flights, ten weeks to extricate dad from Australia and reintegrate him, reintegrate as much as we could from Australia that is, into British life.

One of the things I could never understand about British governmental red-tape was, if dad had moved to live in Spain or Vietnam his state pension would have increased yearly in line with British pensions, but moving to a commonwealth country, like Australia, his pension was frozen at the rate on the day he left the UK. So, one of the things we had to do to reintegrate him was get his pension sorted out. Everything we could do from Australia we did do.

Finally, the day dawned when we would leave Australia. It was an emotional day. I thought I would return, at some point, but dad knew he never would. This was his birthplace, it had become his home. However, he knew that his health was deteriorating and if he didn't go now he'd, likely, never get another chance to return to the UK and he was looking forward to seeing his family again, who would be waiting at the airport for him.

The last few months had been stressful on him, I hoped that once in the air he would relax and enjoy the flight and have a good time back in the UK. The flight was in two stages, Perth to Hong Kong and then Hong Kong to London Heathrow. I had paid the extra to fly business class, partly because of the premium service and priority boarding but mostly for the business class lounges at the airports. The business class seats were a bonus. Dad was pampered by the cabin crew, who pretty much ignored me, and the flights were good for him. He was able to rest, watch a few movies and sleep a bit. The change over at Hong Kong was a bit hectic, as we only had an hour to get to our connecting flight. The airline had assigned someone to help us, so they pushed dad through the crowds, but they didn't speak English, and my Chinese is non-existent. So, asking where the toilets were was met with a glorious smile, a nod, and we were taken to the gate, ready for our next flight. I guess it could have been so much worse.

The second leg of our flight was good too, and the time passed, even though, bizarrely, it did not fly by. But we got to Heathrow and was met by a very nice man who helped us through passport control, baggage claim and customs. Dad's wheelchair had been checked in at Perth, we borrowed a wheelchair from the airline throughout the journey, but when we got to baggage claim there was no wheelchair. The nice airline man said he'd follow-up on it and we could take the airline wheelchair for now. So, with his help we got through all the checks in record time, actually we were simply waved through customs, and finally came out to be greeted by relatives. It was a bit much for dad, who shed a tear.

We were back in the UK, essentially homeless.

5 – Homecoming

On a warm day in August 2015, at about 6pm, our flight from Hong Kong arrived at Heathrow. The flight had been stressful, the rush for the connecting flight had been bad enough but on arrival we discovered dad's wheelchair had been 'mislaid'.

By the time we exited the controlled area and walked into arrivals we were both ready for a cup of tea and a rest, just one more thing to endure… the loving welcome of the family. My brother, John, and his partner were waiting for us. We had been delayed, because of the missing wheelchair, but finally we were reunited. It was emotional but we ended up at a hotel, not far from the airport.

Dad wanted to go straight to his room, he was exhausted, but my brother wanted to have a drink and talk, catch-up and just be with him. Dad, being dad, went off to his room to have a nap and I had to sit and talk to my brother, even though I was also very tired, I can never sleep much on planes.

After an hour or so I went up to dad's room, to see that he was ok, and he was awake and sitting in the tiny armchair reading the complimentary newspaper. He didn't want to go down again. He was still so tired from the journey. It wasn't just that he was tired, he was embarrassed, he hated being seen in a wheelchair, especially by people he knew. Even so, he 'pulled himself together', a phrase he often used, and got ready.

We went down to the hotel restaurant and met the family. By this time my nephew and his girlfriend had also arrived, a surprise they had planned for us. When we got to the restaurant, and saw David, I heard dad say "oh no!" He was shocked and surprised to see him. He loved his grandson and had missed him very much, but dad didn't like surprises like that. He didn't want David to see him in the wheelchair. I stopped wheeling him and we talked about it. Finally, I convinced him that David would see him eventually so it may as well be now. So, with smiles we didn't really feel, we arrived at the table. They had been so engrossed in their own conversation that they hadn't seen us arrive, so they hadn't seen us hesitate before coming over… at least they never mentioned it if they had.

As we were approaching the table dad had been getting more and more uneasy. As soon as we arrived at the table David gave dad a hug and all that unease and anxiety suddenly vanished. It was a lovely moment.

We had a good meal and a delightful conversation. The food was delicious, for hotel food, and the beer had flowed freely, maybe a little too freely. Well, it was a hotel, so it was more expensive than free but there was plenty of it. By midnight dad was struggling to keep awake, although he was enjoying the evening, and I asked him if he wanted to call it a night. I felt awful, like I was spoiling everyone's evening, but dad said that he was ready for bed.

We all said our goodnights and I took dad up to his room. In his room I asked if he'd had a good time and, to my relief, he had. It had been a shock to see them all sitting there, and he had felt like bolting back to the room but was happy he'd stayed and was grateful that David had been there.

We talked for a little while, I showed him the phone and wrote my room number on the notepad next to it, so he'd be able to contact me if he needed me. I asked him again if he needed anything else, but he said he was fine. At this point he was still able to dress and undress himself, it took time but he was determined to cling on to every bit of his independence. So, I said goodnight and went to my room, just down the corridor.

Next morning I went into dad's room, at about 9am. He was up and dressed and had even made himself a cup of tea. I made myself a coffee and we sat for a while talking about the coming day. The plan was for John to drive us down to Plymouth and to spend a few days with us. Back in Australia I was looking at hotels in Plymouth but when John offered to meet us at the airport, drive us to Plymouth and spend a few days with us, dad suggested renting a caravan. I found a beautiful site just outside of Plymouth, at Bovisand.

When we had finished our tea/coffee it was time to go down to breakfast. Reluctantly, dad got into his wheelchair and we went down to the restaurant. We were the last to arrive, John and David, and their respective partners, were there already.

It was a buffet style breakfast, this is where a very busy hotel is a good thing… the fried eggs were fresh. No bouncy rubber eggs for us today! A buffet was a challenge for dad. I wheeled him around while he made his selection. A member of the hotel staff was very helpful, he carried the tray while dad chose what kind of sausage he wanted and whether or not to have baked beans and I loaded his plate, then the member of staff carried the tray to the table. He smiled and disappeared back to work before we could even thank him properly.

We had a long and leisurely breakfast, there was lots of chat, family gossip and talk about the future. After breakfast we went back to our rooms to collect our bags and regrouped at reception. After checking-out David gave dad a huge hug and went off home as he wasn't coming to Plymouth with us. We loaded the car with luggage and started our long drive from London to Plymouth. We made a couple of stops, all the breakfast coffee had to go someplace, but finally found the caravan site. The site was located by the sea, it really was a very beautiful place, just like the website had said, so refreshing that an advert showed reality and not a marketing fantasy.

6 – Caravanning

We checked-in, got the keys and found the caravan. It was a large caravan with a reasonably sized open plan living area and kitchen, a small shower room and toilet and two 'double' bedrooms. The main bedroom was big enough, there was a double bed and a little space to walk around the bed. The second bedroom had two tiny single beds and no room... there were marks on the walls where someone had tried, and failed, to swing a cat.

As a child we had a small caravan and went on caravanning holidays, I hated it. I especially hated having to go to the communal washrooms, or shower block, to use the toilets and wash. At least this caravan had its own facilities, even if there wasn't much space, although I still had flashbacks to those childhood caravanning holidays.

It was late afternoon when we arrived and dad was tired, he needed a nap before we thought about dinner. We needed to get some basics, such as tea, milk and bread, so

John and I went off to find a supermarket and left dad to have his nap.

We found a large Morrison's, a supermarket I had never heard of before, but its range of items was fantastic. I was used to Australian supermarkets such as: Cole's, Woolworth's and Super IGA. Although they had everything you needed, they didn't seem to have quite the range of goods. There was so much I wanted to buy but had to constantly check myself, we only had a small kitchen and an even smaller fridge in the caravan.

It took over an hour to wander around and then we found the small café, so had a quick coffee. We could have taken longer, when we got back to the caravan dad was still asleep. We tried to be quiet but we weren't quiet enough, dad woke up. I put the kettle on, as I knew dad would want a cup of tea, and I wasn't wrong. I had even thought of the biscuits, his favourites, chocolate digestives. It was about 7pm by this time and we were all feeling a little peckish, so over tea we debated what we would have for dinner. John wanted to find a pub that did food, dad didn't mind where we went as long as he could have fish & chips and I thought a take-away and early night would be good. John got his way.

We asked the owner of the caravan site about pubs that did good food and she pointed us towards one just a short drive away, the Mount Batten Hotel, and I must confess, the food was good. The beer was ok too. Like supermarkets, I was used to Australian beer, which is more like lager, but I really like a good bitter or stout.

It was a very pleasant evening, even dad had a good time, just a shame that John had to be the designated driver. There was a sign in the pub advertising their Sunday Carvery, so we said we'd come back on Sunday, and we did, and the carvery was splendid.

We got back to the caravan by 11:45pm and dad went, more or less, straight to bed. John wanted a few beers first, so we took our beers and sat outside. It was a fine night, still warm and the sky was full of stars. By about 12:30 I was ready for bed, so I left John to finish his beers.

Next morning I heard dad getting up, it was about 5:30am, so I got up and put the kettle on. Through his entire adult life dad had the same morning routine. Get up, have three cups of tea with three cigarettes, have breakfast, then wash and he's ready for the day. He had given up smoking, thanks to his COPD, but he still liked his three cups of tea in the morning. We had a lot to plan out, so we got started.

At this point the long-term plan was still for me to get him settled and then I was going back to Australia. So, the paramount concern was to put a roof over his head. In the short-term that meant finding a place to rent, a flat maybe. Once we had a more permanent base we could look to the long-term. However, we both felt the need for a short rest, a break from the stress we'd both been under. To that end, we decided to take a day or two and just be on holiday.

The only concession I made to finding somewhere to live was calling a few estate agents to enquire about rental properties and get on their mailing lists. John got up just after 11am and seemed shocked and hurt that we had already had breakfast.

7 – The Calm Before the Storm

By the time I'd finished with the estate agents, I had no idea just how many estate agents there were in Plymouth, John had finished breakfast. Breakfast! Dad and I were thinking about lunch. Anyway, we were ready to go out and do something. It was a beautiful day, so we decided to have a run into Cornwall.

As a child the family had been to Cornwall on caravanning holidays many times. Some of the happiest memories had been holidays in the small Cornish fishing village of Mevagissey. The caravan site had a stunning location, right on top, at the edge, of the cliffs, with fantastic views. I'm sure you can't do it now, with health and safety ruining everyone's fun, but back in the 1970s you could climb up and down the cliffs. Dad loved to climb down to the harbour from the top of the cliffs. I was terrified and would refuse to go too near the edge, which earned me the nickname 'Windy Whiffle'. Strangely, I'd climb up from the bottom, as long as I didn't look down, if I looked down I'd freeze and dad would have to 'rescue' me.

We visited Mevagissey several times on these caravanning holidays, over the years. On one visit, I remember, we went into a pub (nothing unusual in that!) for a pub lunch. The usual lunch was of the ploughman's kind (a slab of cheese, a bit of crusty bread and some pickle) but this day dad decided to be adventurous and try something he'd never had, smoked mackerel. I had the same. It was a first time for both of us and lead to a lifelong love of the smoked fish. Even today, every time I smell smoked mackerel I think of Mevagissey.

With all that family history, Mevagissey was the obvious choice for the days drive. It was a lovely drive too, dad enjoying the journey through the English countryside. We talked about those family caravanning holidays and the times dad had driven that way working as a lorry driver. It was a good time. When we arrived, much of the little village we remembered looked the same. The harbour was just the same, maybe some new boats. The pubs and shops around the harbour looked familiar, although the names had changed and the type of business may have changed. Some of the little shops were now cafes and the pubs had changed but we did recognise the pub we first had smoked mackerel. So, we went there for lunch.

Oh, joy! They had smoked mackerel on the menu so, in honour of those family caravanning holidays, I had that. Dad had fish and chips, John had been talking about 'real' Cornish pasties throughout the drive, so no one was surprised when that's what he ordered. The food was delicious, simple but delicious. The mackerel was perfect, served with a small salad and fresh crusty bread. They also gave me some horseradish sauce, made, they said, with Cornish clotted cream. I had eaten smoked mackerel many times but that was the first time I'd had horseradish with it… two mackerel firsts in the same place, separated by 40 years! I loved it, now I can't imagine smoked mackerel without the hot sauce accompaniment.

Dad's fish and chips was huge, the cod over-hung the plate on both sides, and it wasn't a small plate, and it was so thick and 'meaty', the fish not the plate. The flesh was pristine white and creamy, just the way he liked it. Other than his family, the good old fish and chips was one of the things he'd missed most living in Australia. Australian fish was fantastic… but it wasn't cod or haddock. There's something special about the fish caught in the cooler waters around the UK and dad had missed that something. The fish at the pub the night before had been ok, he'd enjoyed it, but this was so much better. He had a small appetite but managed to finish all the fish, although most of the chips and a quantity of batter was left behind.

After lunch we had a walk around the harbour. Dad was getting used to the wheelchair, still not happy relying on it, he was resigning himself to needing one. Walking around Mevagissey harbour he was too lost in nostalgia to worry about the wheelchair. He had always loved boats, and we spent a long time looking at the fishing and day boats moored up in the harbour. Looking at the rocky face of the cliffs it still terrified me that we had climbed them, once a windy whiffle always a windy whiffle.

There was time for a quick coffee and then it was time to head back to Bovisand. Dad was getting tired, he'd missed his afternoon nap, so we called it a day. On the drive back dad dozed and I was lost in memory, by the time we got back to the caravan it was early evening and talk turned to dinner. Dad didn't feel like going out again, it had been a big day, and an emotional one. So we decided on a take away from the nearby Indian restaurant and a quiet drink in the caravan, we watched a western on tv.

By 10 o'clock dad was ready for bed, so he retired and left John and I to fill the rest of the night with conversation. I called it a night at around midnight, leaving John to finish the beer.

Next morning was a rerun of the previous morning, dad and I got up early, had three cups of tea and breakfast before John got up late. We decided to visit Plymouth City centre. Both dad and I had to organise bank accounts. For many years before moving to

Australia dad had banked with the Halifax so he was keen to open a new Halifax account, he trusted them.

We found our way to Drake's Circus, the main shopping centre in the heart of the city, and the Halifax branch a short walk from the shopping centre. Unfortunately, we couldn't open accounts straight away, we had to make appointments. We did and then headed off to a Costa Coffee.

I thought I knew Plymouth. Before going to university I'd worked at a school just outside Plymouth and had visited the city many times during my stay at the school but Plymouth had changed so much. I should have expected that, I hadn't been to Plymouth since 1988, in those intervening 27 years I'd changed so why shouldn't the city?

After coffee we did a little shopping. Dad spotted the Marks & Spencer's in Drake's Circus, yet another thing he'd missed in Australia, and so we had a walk around the men's department. Dad bought some socks and a sweater. I went through to the food hall and got some provisions, including some fillet steaks that looked delicious (and, sorry to any vegetarians, they were wonderful, you guys don't know what you're missing). I still had some Australian dollars in my wallet, so was delighted to spot an exchange kiosk in the shopping centre and spent some time in a Waterstone's book shop. Our last stop was to get some pasties, for lunch, and then it was back to the caravan. Dad was looking forward to his afternoon nap and I wanted to start the book I'd bought in Waterstone's.

Dinner was taken care off, I fried the steaks, and some mushrooms I'd picked up in M&S and backed a few jacket potatoes. The steaks were very good but, for me, the best part of the meal was watching John doing the washing up, I cooked so he did the cleaning.

Dad felt like going out that evening, well, he was ok with the idea, so we went out to a pub for a little drink. We left the pub well before closing time, which must have been a first for dad. As a younger man, dad had enjoyed pubs and drinking. He had earned the nickname, 'James Last', not because of his musical ability but rather because he was usually the last person to leave a pub. Back at the caravan we had one more drink and then it was an early night, at least an early night for John, as we had to go back into Plymouth in the morning for our appointments at the Halifax.

In the morning dad was feeling tired and was having trouble catching his breath. This wasn't unusual, he tended to have good and bad days. The bad days tended to come after really good days, on the really good days he would often be more active, it was like his body rebelled after a little exertion, which is probably not far from the truth. The day before he'd felt pretty good, he was still very weak and needed the wheelchair but had been closer to his old self. This morning he appeared shrunken, more shadow than human. It took him a long time to get out of bed and he took longer over his cups of tea but finally he seemed to recover a little and was ready for the trip to the Halifax.

The appointment was pretty painless. Normally, for privacy reasons, they see people individually but in our case they saw us together. It didn't take very long and soon both dad and I had shiny new Halifax accounts. When we finished with the Halifax, dad wanted to go straight back to the caravan.

When we got back he wanted a cup of tea and then went back to bed, saying he was a little tired. He suggested that John and I go out somewhere, his way, I guess, to say we were too noisy and he wanted some peace and quiet. I checked with him that he was alright, and satisfied that he was, John and I went off.

This was the first time John had seen dad on a 'bad' day and he was shocked. He'd been shocked on first seeing dad at the airport but this was so much worse. On his 'good' days, you could catch glimpses of the dad of old, his sense of humour shone through, as did the light in his eyes. The shadow dad on 'bad' days was unrecognisable. This was a bad 'bad' day. I had seen days like this before, so wasn't too worried but John was, for the first time, scared of losing him.

We stayed away for a couple of hours to give dad plenty of time to get some rest. When we got back to the caravan dad was still in bed but awake and, surprise surprise, he was ready for a cup of tea. He also looked a lot better and told us he was feeling better too. Seeing dad looking better reassured John and he calmed down a bit.

Over the next couple of days we did similar things, a couple of day trips to various places, places that held nostalgic importance to us. A drive on to Dartmoor and a visit to Tavistock. Most of the time dad had 'good' days. On the sixth day John was going back to Sheffield. He got up early, had breakfast and packed his bags into the car and off he went. Dad was sad to see him go but it was also a relief, he was 'putting on a good show' for John, he didn't want him to see just how bad he'd been feeling.

8 – It Hits the Fan

John drove away, starting his long journey to Sheffield, midmorning. It was warm and sunny, so we spend the rest of the morning sitting at the little picnic table outside the caravan, looking through estate agent websites. Dad was having a bad day, he was pale and his breathing was very laboured. Just talking was a herculean task but he carried on.

Around 1 o'clock we had lunch, a can of tomato soup and cheese sandwiches. This was a comfort lunch, whenever I was sick as a child mum would give me tomato soup and a cheese sandwich for lunch. When I was sick it was usually Tonsillitis and a bowl of tomato soup and a cheese sandwich (dunked in the soup) was easy to eat and made me feel warm and comfortable. In the family it became the standard, go to, lunch for someone under the weather. Today, dad managed to eat most of the soup but didn't touch the sandwich.

After lunch dad, with my help, went to bed, saying he was going for his afternoon nap. Dad's afternoon naps were sacred, no matter where he was, at home, at work or on holiday, 2pm was nap time. I found it frustrating as a child but it was part of the rhythm of the day. He never liked going to bed for the afternoon nap, though, saying he'd be out for the rest of the day. He liked to sit in his chair, stretch out his legs, one hand cradling his chin and the other tucked into the waistband of his trousers. As soon as he got into that position he was asleep in seconds and, precisely, one hour later he'd wake up, get up and make a cup of tea. He really was precise, when I got a digital watch with a stopwatch function, I timed him a couple of times. It was always an hour, +/- a minute or so, quite remarkable.

Three hours after he'd gone for his nap I heard him stirring, tapped on the door and asked if he was ready for some tea. His voice was very croaky, he asked if I'd come in and give him a hand. I went in and he was lying on the bed. He needed help getting to a sitting position, just that took the breath out of him and he had to sit for a few minutes to recover. Then he was ready to get to his feet and move into the living area. Slowly, we manoeuvred to the sofa in the lounge. He sat down, gasping for breath. This was bad, even for a 'bad' day. I asked him if he wanted to see a doctor or go to hospital, "don't be daft!" was his response. I regret listening to him and not calling for an ambulance but after using one of his inhalers, and sitting for a few minutes, his breathing became easier, so I ignored that little voice in my head, a big mistake!

I was sitting on the sofa, looking worried, watching him. It must have made him very nervous. I was useless, finally dad said where's that tea and my hypnotic trance was broken. I put the television on for him and changed the channel to a movie channel, there was an old western on, Audie Murphy was being a hero. Not one of dad's favourite actors, it was still a western, and he loved westerns. He could have been a contestant on Mastermind with his extensive knowledge of western movies (1940 – 1992).

I made the tea and then started preparing dinner. Dad wanted something light, so I was going to fry some salmon steaks and a little mashed potato. I prepared the fish, peeled the potatoes and left everything so I could cook it when we were ready for dinner. Then sat down and watched the most decorated American GI, Audie Murphy, win the day again on screen.

6 o'clock rolled round and dad said he was ready for dinner. So, I put the potatoes on and, when they were almost ready, started frying the fish, in a little butter with a splosh of white wine vinegar at the end, to cut through the richness of the fish. We ate dinner watching 'The Guns of Navarone'. Dad ate most of his dinner, which helped to reassure me, and as the big guns exploded on screen, I did the washing up. Maybe the only time I missed John!

When the movie finished another one started but it was one we'd seen a few days ago, so we flicked through the channels until we found an old episode of Minder. The process of flicking through channels was repeated until about 10pm when dad said he was ready for bed. I got up to help him but he said he was ok to go by himself.

He slowly headed to the toilet and then said a last goodnight and went to bed.

I turned the tv off and grabbed my phone. Aren't these smartphones both wonderous and terrible? Terrible because you can't escape reminders and emails, and if you lose your phone you've lost so much of your life. Wonderous because you can store all your music and photos on one pocket sized device. I played some music and read the last few chapters of the book I bought in Plymouth a few days before.

Around midnight I was feeling ready for sleep so I stopped the music and walked to the toilet. Coming out of the toilet, which was next to dad's bedroom, I heard him calling for me.

I opened the bedroom door and he was awake, he asked me to open his window. I walked over to the window and drew back the curtain, the window was already open. I told him this, but he didn't reply. I looked over to him and he had just stopped, it was as if someone had simply threw a switch. He slept propped up on a couple of pillows, this helped him breath during the night. When I looked at him now he was sitting up, eyes and mouth open. I couldn't see or hear him breathing.

I took hold of his hand and called to him but there was no response. He was gone. Running back into the loungeroom I regressed back into a scared little boy, I grabbed the phone and, in my panic, dialled '000', the Australian emergency number. I quickly realised my error and cancelled the call and redialled the correct '999', asked for an ambulance, gave my name and the address of the caravan park.

The person on the other end of the line was fantastic, she spoke to me in an authoritative and calm voice. She talked me through putting dad into the recovery position and… the rest is a haze. I know that dad did come round, I had thought he was dead but he must have just been deeply unconscious.

When he came back to consciousness I hugged him and he was confused and disorientated, and a little annoyed that I'd woken him from a beautiful sleep. He was even more annoyed when the ambulance arrived. The paramedics came into the caravan, all professionalism and activity, and I was unceremoniously ushered out. They hooked him up to a portable ECG and oxygen, put him on a stretcher and bundled him into the ambulance. They told me it looked like a heart attack and they were taking him to Derriford Hospital and did I want to come with him. I did, so I just grabbed my phone and wallet and slammed the caravan door.

The drive to Derriford Hospital felt like hours, in reality it was only about 30 minutes, all the while dad looking, accusingly, at me and asking why I had done this. Finally, we arrived and was rushed into the emergency department.

9 – Derriford Hospital

When we arrived at the accident and emergency department there was an initial flurry of activity. Doctors, young and old, and countless nurses bustled around him. They fitted a canula, took so much blood, hooked him up to various machines, prodded and poked… and then disappeared, leaving us alone in a cubicle, for hours. After what seemed a geological age, a nurse came, hurriedly, in and connected a saline drip, saying dad was very dehydrated, then left again. Not too long after this someone else came in, clipboard in hand, and asked lots of questions. We were then left alone for a long time.

Dad asked me why I had called an ambulance. I tried to explain what had happened, that he had just stopped talking, moving and, even, breathing. He didn't respond to me and I was sure he had died. Then he told me what it had been like for him.

He remembered calling me and asking for the window to be opened. As I pulled the curtains back he saw bright, flashing, twinkling lights all around the window. Then everything went dark and he didn't know anything until I put him in the recovery position, not that he knew that was what I was doing, all he knew was that I was moving him. He thought he'd just been in a very deep sleep, it had been a good sleep, sound and deep, and he had been very upset that I'd disturbed him.

After about two hours waiting, dad needed to use the toilet. I pressed the button, and we waited, then I went out to look for someone. Now, I know everyone was busy but aren't they supposed to be busy helping patients? This is called the National Health Service, shouldn't they be busy providing that Service?

When I approached someone sitting at a computer they informed me they were far too busy, I approached a group of people, who were apparently talking about going for a drink at the weekend, but they tried to ignore me until they realised I wasn't going anywhere. Finally, one of the group turned to me and I got the help dad needed. Going back to the cubicle, no one had responded to the button I'd pressed, I saw dad anew. He looked so small and, somehow, reduced. For a moment I thought I'd gone to the wrong cubicle, the sight was so shocking, so very heart breaking.

Here was a man who was weak, so weak he couldn't push himself up the bed, he kept slipping down. He had been so strong and active. A man who climbed up and down rocky cliffs, a man who never backed down from a challenge, a man who struggled, in agony, to work because it was his duty. And here was the merest echo of that man.

He had never looked so small and scared but was still trying to be brave, he was trying to make jokes with the nurse. I left the cubicle while the nurse helped him go to the toilet. I left the cubicle, ostensibly, to give dad some privacy but also so he didn't see the tears in my eyes. Waiting outside the cubicle I overheard dad talking to the nurse, he talked about wasting their time and that he shouldn't be there, it was only his over reacting son. When he'd finished the nurse came out, looked at me as if I was the spilled contents of the bedpan, and said that he was finished and I could go back in.

I sat with him for several more hours, he managed to doze but there was far too much noise and activity going on around us. One person, in a nearby cubicle, was experiencing tremendous pain and discomfort, their screams were echoing around the department. The screaming went on and on, part of me felt something should be done to ease this person's suffering and another part, I'm ashamed to confess, just wished they'd be quiet. Worrying about the suffering of a loved one can make us more callous of the suffering of strangers.

Time had lost meaning but, at some point, a doctor came in to see us and said that dad would be taken for a scan and x-ray. More time passed and he was taken for the scans. I waited. After the scans were completed we were taken back to emergency but had to wait in the corridor, the cubicle had been given to another visitor to this purgatory.

Finally, a doctor came looking for dad and explained that he had, indeed, had a massive heart attack and he'd need to be admitted to the cardiac ward. We were 'lucky', obviously their definition of the word 'lucky' was very different to mine, there was a bed available on a cardiac ward and dad would be transferred there when the paperwork was completed. What really holds the NHS together is red tape!

It wasn't until a long time after all this that I could appreciate just how lucky we really were. Talking to other people who had cared for loved ones in Derriford, I heard terrible stories of patients being put on surgical wards and pressured to go home too soon, as beds were at such a premium.

The person doing the paperwork was a very slow typist, as we waited another three hours before an orderly arrived to move dad up to the ward. The orderly was one of the few people we'd met at the hospital who treated dad as a person and not an accumulation of symptoms. I regret not seeing this orderly's name, I would have liked to thank him.

10 – On the Ward

The ward was a hive of activity, medical staff rushing around, everyone looking very busy… how could any patient rest with all this activity going on? The orderly said his goodbyes and wished dad a speedy recovery and he, too, rushed off to help someone else. We were left talking to a nurse, who looked at dad's notes. She asked if he wanted a single room, I didn't know the NHS offered those. Dad was a very social person, so he wasn't sure but I looked around and suggested he might be able to rest more in a private room, it's what I would have wanted.

We were taken to the room, it was certainly private, it was also very cold. The nurse gave some reason for why the room was kept so cold, and got dad into the bed and left, promising to be right back with a nebuliser and some tea. She didn't return, like in A&E, they were very busy but if they say they'll do something I think they should do it. After a while I went in search of someone to give him the nebuliser and a cup of tea, and an extra blanket.

Dad said he didn't like the room so, when a doctor arrived to go over his notes and ask the same slew of questions, I told the doctor dad didn't like the room, it was too cold for him. I expected the doctor to say there weren't any beds on the ward and he'd have to wait until a bed became available but he said he'd get him moved right away. I would think most people put into that room made the same request.

When the doctor left, almost immediately two people came in to move dad onto the main ward. He was much happier there, he had someone to talk to and it was much warmer. The noise wasn't a problem, he could sleep through most things. He was very tired, he'd been through a lot and hadn't been able to get much sleep so once he was settled on the ward I left him to rest. I had a lot to do, there were things he needed and, I have to admit, I was drained too.

I got back to the caravan and put the kettle on but was asleep before it boiled. As soon as I sat down I realised just how tired, exhausted, I was. When I woke up I felt guilty that I had fallen asleep so readily while dad needed so much in hospital, but I wouldn't be any help to him if I was exhausted. I collected the bits and pieces he would need, his shaver, pyjamas, a dressing gown, his false teeth and such, and went back to the hospital.

When I arrived my first stop was the little Marks & Spencer food store next to the entrance to the hospital. I realised I hadn't eaten anything, so I bought a couple of M&S prawn sandwiches. I also spotted some Victoria plums, dad loved Victoria plums. When my brother married his second wife they moved into a house with an ancient, and very large, Victoria plum tree in the garden. I'd never had plums like them and have never had any like them since. Rich, juicy and sweet, they were the biggest plums I'd ever seen too. One of those plums was equal to about three of these M&S plums but these were Victoria plums so they might, at the very least, bring back a pleasant memory.

I also popped into the hospital shop, on my way to the lifts, to get the obligatory

Robinson's Barley Water (lemon). When I arrived on the ward I must have looked like a beardless Santa Claus, large sack of goodies in tow. Dad was asleep when I arrived so I just sat in the chair next to his bed and ate one of my prawn sandwiches, wishing I'd bought a coffee. A nurse walked by and stopped to talk to me, he asked if I was his son and would I like a cup of tea, it was almost time for the tea trolley to come by. He also said I could give him a prawn sandwich, I was going to do that anyway, they were his favourite, I wonder how he knew. As he was talking the tea trolley came along and, as if smelling the tea, dad woke up and smiled at me. He looked so much better, still very pale, withdrawn and so small, why do hospitals seem to shrink people? However, compared to how he looked in A&E he looked the picture of health.

He may have looked better but he was still very weak, the moment he tried to drink his tea, and his hand shook so badly he couldn't raise the cup to his mouth, it was obvious just how bad he was. I helped him hold the cup and he drank some tea, he hated it. He hated the fact that I had to helped him do something so simple, normal, so every day. The smile he greeted me with on first waking had gone, now he was close to tears. He felt he was just a burden and that was exactly what he didn't want. He also thought the tea was terrible. I couldn't do anything about the tea, but I did try to reassure him about burdens. He wasn't a burden; I could never consider him a burden, 'he ain't heavy, he's my father!'

When I was 14 we had a family holiday in Malta: mum, dad, John, Kath (John's then wife) and I. It was a lovely holiday until, about half-way through, mum suddenly died during the night of a heart attack. It was a terrible shock and dad suffered greatly, we all felt numb, but he never once abdicated his role as father to an obnoxious teenager. He never complained and he never called me a burden, although I must have been. Looking back at those days, I was truly a horrible teenager. It wasn't until I was an adult that I really understood just how wonderful he had been and how tough it must have been for him.

So, how could he think he was a burden to me now. I was more than happy to be there for him, to help him in any way I could. No, 'happy' was not the right word, I was far from happy about what was happening. It was more like honoured, it was an honour and a privilege to be able to give this wonderful, fantastic, man, my dad, something back. I'd have no more talk about burdens. So, now drink your terrible tea and here, here's a prawn sandwich. Although terrible, the tea did cheer him up, or maybe it was the sarnie. Dad said that, an hour or so, before I came in he was told a doctor would come by to speak with him. We waited.

Being in hospital is not just about getting well, it's all an exercise in waiting. You wait for a nurse to come over, you wait to see a doctor, you wait for meals, you wait for procedures, you wait to go home. Going home is a major topic of conversation: "when are you going home?", "I'm going home in a few days", "you can go home tomorrow." Many patients look forward to going home, with beds at such a premium, the staff look forward to patients going home too, but what about patients who don't have a home to go to.

While we waited for the doctor to visit, we discussed the issue of a home. It had always been our plan to find somewhere to rent, a flat or small house, but the heart attack had pushed that up the 'todo' list, and added a few items too. The original plan was to do some holidaying first but now it was urgent that a suitable rental was found. The caravan was fine for a holiday, but it was not ideal for convalescence. We discussed the must haves for a place to live, things such as access, location, stairs, etc. As we discussed these things the doctor arrived.

Dad listened to what the doctor had to say, although I don't think he really heard much, he was overloaded by the whole experience. The doctor said that they wanted to do some more scans, what they really wanted to do was an angiogram but, unfortunately, they felt dad was too weak. They had also found his kidneys were not functioning properly and the dyes used in the procedure would put too much stress on already failing organs. They had also seen some 'shadows' on his lungs.

Dad explained that he had a history of pneumonia and pneumonia left its marks on the lungs, but the doctor said these shadows were different. Ideally, they'd perform a biopsy to remove all doubt but, again, dad was too weak to undergo such a procedure. Basically, they were limited in what they could do, so they were limited in what they could know for sure. However, they had good reason to believe that the shadows on his lungs were cancerous and that they were reasonably advanced. There was little they could do, other than provide palliative care and, with a smile, she asked if there were any questions, we were shocked and couldn't think of anything to ask, so she said goodbye and left.

I made an excuse and went after her. I caught up with her in the corridor and asked her a few questions relating to prognosis and what we could expect to happen. I already had a fair idea. The prognosis was not good. He was elderly, had failing kidneys, a heart condition, COPD and lung cancer (said with such confidence and finality that they had no doubt the shadows were cancer), there was no coming back from this. There would be a rapid downward progression in his health and death in six to twelve months. I was both shocked at her candour and thankful for her honesty. I was very thankful I hadn't asked these questions in front of dad. He was brave, stoic in the face of suffering, but he did tend to the 'glass half empty' way of thinking, and I didn't want him dwelling on such a timetable. Thanking the doctor, I turned, took a deep breath, put on my best 'happy' smile and went back to sit with dad.

The next few days were a haze of rushing to get things organised for his homecoming and getting to the hospital to spend plenty of time with dad, I felt it was important to be with him as much as possible. The last thing I wanted was for him to be alone and brooding.

The many estate agents were sympathetic to the situation, but only one really understood the urgency. She was able to find a nice flat, near the Barbican, that we could move into virtually immediately. Our circumstances were a little unusual, no references or rental history, but it's amazing what six months rent in advance can do to ease any landlord misgivings. I signed the contract, parted with some cash, and became the proud tenant of a flat. That was a huge relief, dad would have a home to come to. The only slight problem was the flat was unfurnished.

The furniture options available today is mindboggling, so many retailers all offering the 'best' range and the 'best' prices, "sale ends Sunday!" sort of thing. The only problem is that delivery times for many of these options is measured weeks, if not months. Dad could be discharged at any time now, so I needed delivery times measured in hours. That limits the choices considerably, which was actually a good thing. It made deciding much easier.

It was a busy time, but everything was in place by the time dad was discharged. He left the hospital not really knowing where he was going but as he entered the flat he saw a home and he was able to relax. Everything he needed was there for him, he had a comfy chair to watch tv from, and have his naps in, and a firm bed to sleep in. He always liked firm beds, softer beds gave him back pain. I had even put some pictures he liked on the walls. It was a home.

11 – Coming Home

The last couple of weeks had been hectic, I had lived two lives, that of hospital visitor and, a totally different life, that of frenetic shopper. It felt as if I'd been to every shop in Plymouth, buying a complete home, that usually takes years, in just two weeks. When dad was discharged and got home life settled into a routine. Without the daily visits to Derriford Hospital my life became more domestic.

One of the first things we had to do after dad arrived home was sign on with a General Practitioner, the doctor's surgery we used in Australia was a bit far to go to for an emergency appointment, and we may be outside their catchment area anyway. In such situations Google is your friend. Online I found many GP surgeries, but Friary House Surgery had some good reviews, so I booked us in for an introductory appointment.

The surgery is a large one, with several doctors, many of whom come and go, but there is a core group of doctors who are partners in the practice, so they remain constant. We met with one of the partners, Dr Tuckley, who remained dad's doctor throughout his illness. During this introductory meeting the doctor said, and did, something the significance of which was totally lost on me at the time, although much later I realised just how important it had been. He mentioned the name "St. Luke's" and said he'd refer dad to them. At that time I hadn't even heard of St Luke's but would change, in time.

He also reviewed dad's notes, took a medical history, verbally as it would take time to get his notes from Australia, and set up his medication regime. He then organised for a district nurse to visit dad at home. I was very impressed with the surgery and Dr Tuckley. Friary House Surgery have a fantastic system for booking appointments. You call the surgery, as for any surgery, and tell the receptionist what you need. Then, usually within an hour or two, a doctor will call back and triage your situation. You are then given an appointment based on the doctor's medical opinion. Whenever I called for an appointment, dad saw a doctor that day. It worked very well.

A few days after our first appointment with Dr Tuckley I received a telephone call from St Luke's Hospice. I was very ignorant about what modern hospices do for the community. I always thought I understood what a hospice was, it was a special kind of hospital that catered for those close to death. So, although dad had lung cancer he wasn't in the last stages, what could a hospice do for us now? I have since been educated.

A hospice, like St Luke's, does provide specialised medical care for patients in the latter stages of terminal illness but they provide so much more, most of what they provide isn't in the hospice, it's in the community, in patient's homes. So much of their work is directed at allowing patients to remain at home.

That first phone call introduced me to Paul who was going to be dad's palliative care nurse. He wanted to arrange a visit, to meet dad and introduce himself. We set up a day and time for him to visit. Four or five days later Paul arrived.

Dad liked Paul right from the start. His mix of empathy and professionalism was just right. He was friendly and forthright, he didn't try to hide anything. He was direct but in a friendly and pleasant way. What he told us wasn't pleasant but he told us in a way that wasn't cold or uncaring. He had obviously done this kind of thing before. He also offered us so much general information, showing us what support was available to us. He asked if we needed carers to help with dad's general care?

Dad was weak, his mobility was very limited, but he was still dressing and washing himself and he was able to walk from bedroom to living room to toilet. Yes, it took him a long time to do those things and he got very tired doing them, but he wanted to carry on doing them for himself. The idea of having carers, strangers, coming in to help him with these things was horrifying to him.

So, we declined the offer but Paul said carers were available when or if we needed them in the future. He also suggested a few things that would make life just a little bit easier. He organised a shower stool, so dad could sit while showering. There was another stool, to sit in the hallway, so dad could sit and rest if he needed when walking from the bedroom to the living room. Dad tended to spend most of the day sitting in his chair, watching tv or napping, so Paul ordered a cushion designed to prevent pressure sores. Finally, he got us a frame that encircled the toilet, giving the toilet sturdy arms dad could use to help getting on and off the toilet. All things I wouldn't have instantly thought of but once mentioned were so obvious.

Paul was a prescribing palliative nurse, he was able to prescribe medication and became an important interface between us and the medical profession. He visited regularly, at the start it may have been every three or four weeks but as our need increased so did his visits. I also had his telephone number, so if there were any issues, big or small, I could call him. If needed he'd come over as soon as he could, otherwise he could provide information over the phone or liaise with other medical professionals. Paul, and St Luke's generally, became the keystone of dad's care.

Caring for a terminally ill person involves a great deal of talking to medical professionals, dealing with medications and generally being a pseudomedic (unpaid). You become expert in the condition(s) and medications the person you care for has. Much of your time, even when away from the terminally ill person, is given over to worrying about them, but medicine, and health care, is not the only things in life.

Dad settled into a routine he became very comfortable with and I had my routine. Both his and my routines were synchronised. The day started early, dad had always been an early riser, he liked to get up at around 5am, so I also liked to get up then too. I'd usually hear him struggling to get up, go to the toilet and get dressed. I learnt very quickly that he didn't want help with this, so while he was doing this I'd go into the kitchen and put the kettle on. It would take dad some time to get ready so I had plenty of time to make the tea.

When he finally got to the living room I had the tv on, so we could watch the news, and a cup of tea ready for him. I'd drink coffee, I needed the caffeine just to stay awake, I wasn't a natural early riser, and we'd watch the early morning news together. Over the next hour or two I'd make another two cups of tea.

After his third cup of tea dad would start the journey back to the toilet and then he'd wash himself. After his ablutions he'd sit on the bed for a long time, recovering from the exertion of washing. Then he'd come back to the living room, where I'd have prepared his breakfast. He was a man of very specific tastes, breakfast had to be either Weetabix, Readybrek or real porridge, and occasionally Cornflakes. He didn't like the same thing too often, so everyday was something different.

This was the time for his first round of medication. I had a system to ensure no medications were missed. Some of his medicines had to be taken once a day, some twice a day, three times a day and four times a day. Some taken as required but do not exceed a specific number of doses. The responsibility of managing someone else's medication is great, missing medication or taking too much might have significant repercussions. My system for managing the medication worked well for me. I listed all of dad's medications on a spreadsheet. Across the page were the times the medications were to be taken. Each week I would print seven of these sheets and keep them with the medicines. As I gave dad a medication I'd tick off that dose on the sheet.

The list was useful as a check that all medications had been taken at the correct times of day but it was useful for other things too. Many medical professionals visited dad, often they asked what medication dad was on. I was able to show them the checklist.

After breakfast he'd have his morning nap. He often said that he got up early so he had time for a morning nap. This would be around 9am, and I would take this opportunity to go out for a walk, maybe go for a coffee or just a walk around the Barbican or Hoe.

To start with I felt a little guilty taking time for myself like this but Paul reassured me that it was so important for carers to look after themselves. I hadn't labelled myself as a carer until then, I was just looking after my dad. I, for some reason, struggled against the label, but I had been a carer for a long time, maybe not a full-time carer, but ever since dad's COPD had got to the point he wasn't able to get about as well as he used to by himself, I had been a carer, although I never thought of myself as one. Now I was a full-time carer, I had been labelled.

The label 'carer' takes over your life. In a very real sense you cease to be 'you', the independent, autonomous 'you' and slowly discover your sole identity is dictated and shaped by the relationship with the person you are caring for. If you are not careful you might lose yourself in the label and never find yourself again. Taking small 'time-outs', like a morning walk around the Barbican, can help to remind you that you are still 'you'.

Even while taking time out you may discover that, above all else, you are a carer, it's almost impossible to forget. While walking around the beautiful Barbican or Hoe in Plymouth I'd find myself thinking about dad, that little voice in my head would, apparently out of nowhere, say "Is he ok?" or "Does he need anything?" and, if I saw something interesting, "Oh, he'd like this!" I usually took my camera with me, both the Barbican and Hoe are very picturesque. One day I found myself taking lots of photos of a row of classic motorcycles parked on the Barbican, I don't even like motorcycles. I was only taking the photos because dad loved motorcycles, especially old British makes. He used to own a Norton Dominator and there was one of those parked on the Barbican.

I'd usually get back to the flat at around 10 or 11am. Sometimes dad was awake, and watching tv, and sometimes he'd still be asleep. If he was asleep he'd wake up soon after I got back, I'd be quiet but he seemed to sense my presence. Then it was tea time, elevenses. He liked to have elevenses as it broke the morning up, that way he could get a pre-lunch nap in. We'd have a cup of tea, occasionally, and I do mean occasionally, dad would have a coffee, and a small snack; something like a crumpet or a couple of biscuits.

During elevenses we'd talk about what to have for lunch and dinner. After elevenses I'd go out again to do the shopping. I liked to go shopping every day, partly to get fresh food but mostly as an excuse to get out of the flat again. I'd usually go to the local Tesco or Sainsbury's mini supermarket but often I'd go to the Plymouth covered market, especially if we wanted fresh fish.

While I was shopping, dad would be sleeping or watching tv. When I got back I'd prepare lunch. Dad usually just wanted a sandwich of some kind, and we'd eat lunch together. We'd talk about whatever was on his mind. Sometimes that was current affairs and politics, he was fascinated by Trump's presidential campaign, sometimes it was what I saw on my walk that morning. The two main topics of conversation were family history, dad was spending more and more time thinking about the old days, and his medical symptoms, he was increasingly obsessed by his condition and would talk about his bodily functions, something he'd have found impossibly embarrassing before. It was also time for his second round of medication, some of his medicines had to be taken after food, some before food and one with food, as if juggling all those medicines wasn't complex enough!

After lunch we'd have another cup of tea and then, at around 2pm, dad would take his afternoon nap. While he was napping I'd do any laundry and make his bed, and then read for a while. Depending on what we had decided on for dinner, I might start preparing dinner.

He'd wake up around 3 or 4pm, his stopwatch accurate one-hour naps were a thing of the past, and have, guess what… a cup of tea and a slice of cake. Then he'd watch a movie on tv, usually a western, if we could find one. After the movie we'd watch the news and then, at around 6:30pm, have dinner. This lead into the evening, where we'd watch some more tv, or a movie if we could find one (or I'd recorded one) until about 10pm, when dad would have a cup of hot chocolate or Horlicks and a final round of medication. Then dad went to go to bed.

12 – Changes

The routine was flexible, some days it had to be changed in order to accommodate a visit from a district nurse, a doctor or Paul. There was also visits from occupational therapists and other sundry medical professionals. One day Paul visited, it started just like all of his previous visits and then he told us he had something to say.

He'd applied for, and got, a new job. A more senior job with another organisation. He told us he'd see us again before he left, he just wanted to tell us in plenty of time, and he assured us that dad's care would still be managed by St Luke's, who would assign another nurse to dad. Dad was more disturbed by this news than I thought he would be, he'd grown accustomed to Paul and he enjoyed Paul's visits. He was worried about having to get used to a new person. He was still happy for Paul, as was I, Paul deserved to promotion. Paul's replacement was a nurse named Sue. She was wonderful too, just as professional and compassionate as Paul, with an equally good sense of humour, although a different kind of humour. After a few visits dad was just as comfortable with Sue as he'd been with Paul.

We had been living in the flat for about three months. I didn't think too much about time passing but with the change from Paul to Sue I realised that three months was a milestone, of a sort. Back in Derriford one of dad's doctors had told me dad might only have six to twelve months left. We were already halfway through the lower estimate. I started to watch dad very closely, to see if I could distinguish any changes in his condition.

He was still doing a lot for himself, even if it took him a long time to do those things and he got so out of breath doing them. Saying he got out of breath doesn't come close to describing what he actually went through. Getting out of breath is an everyday thing, we all get out of breath. Walking up a hill, climbing a few flights of stairs, running for the bus, doing such things we all get out of breath. Usually, a few gasps and a couple of minutes and it's all forgotten. What dad went through many times a day was several orders of magnitude worse. Imagine you had just run a six-minute mile, instead of letting you rest to catch your breath, you are then put into a vacuum chamber and all the air is pumped out. You are already out of breath but now you struggle to breath and just can't get any precious oxygen. You feel as if you are suffocating, that you are dying because of lack of oxygen, you try to relax but your body's instinct for self-preservation has taken over and you just struggle more. It's a torture of agony, and dad went through that several times a day, for things as simple as just having a quick shower or even putting on his socks.

It was a torture for me too, watching him repeatedly go through this and knowing there was nothing I could do. He had inhalers and a nebuliser but these didn't help him when he was in this condition. He just had to suffer until the 'episode' ended. These 'episodes' might last two minutes to five or six minutes, they must have felt like hours to dad. And over the last three months I noticed that these 'episodes' were becoming more frequent and lasted longer.

Strong evidence that his condition was deteriorating.

It was also getting harder and harder to get him to eat enough. His appetite had reduced drastically, at the end of most meals I found half the food left on his plate. You can lead a father to food but you can't make him eat. I couldn't force feed him, all I could do was ensure that the food I presented to him was food he liked and cajole him into eating more. Sue suggested that instead of milk on his breakfast cereal I use a meal supplement. There was a range of ready-made supplements available just for the ill and elderly, they come in tins. Just shake them, open them and consume. I tried various flavours on his cereal and he refused to eat more than a spoonful, the supplements were far too sweet for him and thick, even when mixed with normal milk.

I gave up trying to get him to eat more at mealtimes, I gave him more high calorie snacks throughout the day, two crumpets instead of one, four biscuits instead of two, a bigger slice of cake. Maybe the high sugar and fat content of these things were not a great diet but the doctor was ok with it, dad needed the calories just to keep him going through the day. Ensuring he had enough to eat became an obsession.

One of his favourite things was jellied eels, although he was born in Australia he grew up in a working class area in the Eastend of London and there jellied eels were a popular meal. They were a weekly treat for the family and he still loved them. I scoured every purveyor of fresh fish in the area and finally found tubs of jellied eels in Morrison's. I bought a couple of tubs and presented them to him. He was excited about seeing them again but, sadly, when he tried them, they were just not the same as he remembered. I tried them and I have to confess, I agreed. The jelly was the same but the small slices of eel seemed thinner than I remembered and the flesh was a lot tougher. I don't know who was more disappointed, him or me!

I remember going to seafood stalls, both by the coast while on holiday and in London, usually on a Sunday after a lunchtime drink, and having jellied eels with dad.

They were soft and sweet, the flesh just dropping off the bone. These eels, from Morrison's, were pale imitations. I felt so bad for dad, the excitement of seeing them and the disappointment after trying them.

I did have one seafood success, although it was hard work for me. Another of his favourites was oysters. While living in Australia I took dad to Singapore for a week. I was attending a conference but it was only a two day conference, so we'd had a few days to enjoy this fascinating city together. The hotel, the Shangri La, had the most amazing restaurants, including one with a seafood buffet, oyster bar included. Dad visited the oyster bar again and again. I lost count of the number of oysters he had but the number was impressive, I was reminded of one of those competitive eaters you see on American tv shows. I had half a dozen, and they were delicious. So, when I saw that the fish monger's in the undercover market in Plymouth had oysters I had to get him a dozen.

I got back to the flat at around noon, and when dad saw the oysters he decided to have an early lunch. I didn't have a shucking knife so had to use my Swiss Army knife, it was slow, hard and messy work, but I got through all 12 oysters and dad ate the lot and loved them.

Minor, seafood based, successes a side, dad's appetite was a worry. I found that using larger plates was a good way to get him to eat. Seeing the same amount of food on a larger plate tricks the mind into thinking it is less food, as you see more of the plate, to consume. Giving him small snacks more often throughout the day also worked to get him to eat more, however he remained very slim. He'd always been slim but had also been muscular, now he was slim but had lost a lot of the muscle, he was looking very frail, far frailer than he had three months before.

His condition was very obviously deteriorating but the decline was a bit slower than was originally feared. I did discuss it with his GP and he agreed, he reset the clock back to six months to a year from now. That was a cheery conversation!

Over the last three months I had been looking for a more permanent home. The flat we currently rented was on a six-month contract. The area was pretty good, right in the heart of Plymouth, near the Barbican, located in Moon Street, just behind the Jury's Inn Hotel, a city centre hotel. It was great to get to the shops and was good for visitors, the bus station was, at this time, just around the corner, the train station was a couple of minutes taxi ride and there were bus stops one minute away. However, the flat had its problems. It was on the fifth floor and, although the lift was very reliable, dad didn't like being so high. The fire alarm went off regularly, often in the middle of the night. And the boiler had also been a little temperamental and the landlord was not keen on getting a replacement. So, I searched for a flat or small house to buy.

I saw a number of properties, many of the houses were not right, there were damp issues, location issues, problems with steps and some properties simply required too much work to make them habitable. Finally, one estate agent asked if I'd considered a new build property. I hadn't but was interested.

I went to view a new build flat in Devonport and it seemed to tick all the boxes. It was on the ground floor, access was good, location was ok, no damp problems and it had vacant possession, so as soon as the legal stuff was completed we could move in.

I showed all the brochures and photos I'd taken to dad and he seemed to like it, so I signed on the dotted line and committed to buy a new build flat. The legal process took a little longer than I had originally thought but by the time the rental agreement was due to be renewed on the Moon Street flat, everything was ready on the new flat.

Sue, from St Luke's, suggested that before we moved in one of her colleagues should come and look at the flat and make some suggestions that might make life a bit easier. Although dad was still able to get from the bedroom to the living room by himself he was having problems. Even things like getting out of bed was a struggle.

I met Sue's colleague at the flat and she did make some suggestions, the main one was getting dad a hospital bed. She explained the benefits of this and, although I agreed with her, I felt I needed to discuss it with dad first. Making his bedroom look more like a hospital room might not be what he wanted. When I got back to the Moon Street flat I discussed it with dad and, to my surprise, he was happy with the idea. So we organised a hospital bed delivery, together with a table for the bed. When it arrived I was a little envious, it was all electric. At the touch of a button you could change so many aspects of the bed, including lowering or raising the bed so dad could get in and out of bed easier. I just wanted to lay on it and pretend to be Homer Simpson… "Bed goes up, bed goes down!"

The move to the new flat went very smoothly, the minimum of stress for dad, although quite stressful for me. The removals company were very good. They understood about dad and his medical condition. The morning of the move started just like any other day. Dad got up, did his usual routine and by around 9:30, when the movers arrived, dad was sitting in his chair ready for his morning nap.

I had arranged with the removal firm to move the bedrooms and a couple of boxes from the kitchen and living room but to leave the tv, dad's chair, kettle and a couple of mugs. That way I could get everything moved while dad rested. The movers and I got to the new flat and emptied the truck and filled the bedrooms. I made sure that, although chaos was everywhere, there was a chair ready for dad to sit and a tv he could watch.

I got back to the old flat after about an hour, dad was napping in his chair but when the movers and I came in dad woke up. I made a round of tea for everyone and the packet of biscuits I'd left on the counter was consumed. While we were having tea I called for a taxi and I got dad ready to travel. Then I left with dad, the movers were left to pack and move the few remaining things, dad's armchair, a tv, kettle and sundry items.

By the time the movers arrived at the new flat dad was settled in his bedroom chair watching 'Homes Under the Hammer'. I said goodbye to the movers and got stuck in to organising the living room. The furniture was put into an initial position, as I knew that I would probably have to move things around later, because dad would not like the way I'd placed things, but it was good enough to be able to move dad into so I could get his bedroom sorted out, my bedroom could wait.

With dad dozing in the living room I put his clothes in the wardrobes and draws, organised his medications and medical equipment and generally tidied his room so he could go to bed that night in an orderly and comfortable room. Then I started organising the kitchen, making sure everything was ready to start preparations for dinner. After that I was ready for a coffee and a rest, so I just closed the door to my bedroom, that could wait.

13 – The Impossible Question

We settled into our new life in the new flat, and the new life was pretty much the same as the old. I still had my walks, dad still had his countless cups of tea and naps and we still had numerous visitors of the medical persuasion. The flat itself was ok, there were lots of snags, small problems left by the builders. Some not so small. However, it was light, airy and, most importantly for dad, on the ground floor.

The flat had two bedrooms, the main bedroom was a reasonable size with its own shower room. Dad had that one. My room was little more than a box room but it was just big enough. Dad's room had the hospital bed and table, a chair, chest of draws with a tv on it and sundry medical items, such as a nebuliser. Dad had always liked boats and the sea, so I got some suitable pictures for the walls.

Although the room did look a little like a hospital room it was comfortable and he was happy with it, the pictures of boats at sea, and a few family photos in frames, made it look a little more homely for him. He liked having the en-suite, he'd only ever had one of those in hotels.

The walk from the bedroom to the living room was roughly the same as in the old flat and he was still managing that walk pretty well when we first moved in but after a few weeks it became obvious he was struggling progressively more. He started to use the hall stool, which sat about halfway from bedroom and living room, and he spent longer and longer sitting on the stool.

He was still managing to wash and dress himself, and to use the toilet unaided, but it was taking him longer, with more rest stops, and the recovery time was getting substantially longer, it was devastating to have to standby, doing nothing, while I watched him struggle for breath. It was more devastating still when he would say, after he'd recovered his breath, that he wished I'd let him die in the caravan. He'd always been a 'glass half empty' kind of person but that slight tendency to the dark side had developed to depression and, considering everything that had happened to him, that was very understandable.

Once, and only once, he asked me to help him end his life. He felt he'd got to a point where his quality of life was so poor that death would be preferable. Unless you've had a loved one ask you to do that you have no idea just how terrible it is. I knew he was suffering, the agony he suffered after even the slightest exertion, was heart-breaking but I also saw the good times. When he talked about the old times and we'd both laugh at his exploits. When a western film came on the tv and his eyes lit up because he'd not seen it for years, or even better, a western movie was shown that he'd never seen (a very rare occurrence but it did happen). He was not in constant pain, yes he suffered when he exerted himself, even slightly, but for the majority of time he was pain free.

I'm ashamed to have to admit that I was also concerned about the consequences of helping him end his life. No matter how you phrase it, assisting someone commit suicide was illegal and it came with significant penalties.

I was also selfish, I just wasn't ready to lose him. My entire life was now dedicated to his care. It was like tunnel vision, I was focused on dad and nothing else, nothing in the periphery. Before the COPD, heart attack, failing kidneys and cancer my life was filled with work, friends, travel, now the only thing I could focus on was dad and his wellbeing. I loved him and didn't want to see him go just yet but a part of me was worried about what I'd do without him. I had surrendered my identity, my sense of self, and fully adopted and integrated the identity of 'carer'. What would I do without that? I have spoken to a number of ex-carers and many of them experienced the same thing.

Dad must have understood the difficult position he'd put me in because he told me to forget he'd asked but how can you forget being asked something like that? Even now I sometimes wake up, in the middle of the night, sweating about being asked that impossible question. He never asked again, although he did say he wished he'd died in the caravan many times.

Over the next few months, dad's last months, he suffered a great deal, mostly in terms of attacks to his dignity and independence, but he also experienced many joyful times too. If he'd ended his life when he asked me, he'd have missed out on so much, so many funny, joyful and happy moments. Is that just the way I justify and live with the decision not to help him or did the good moments really outweigh the bad? I really do feel I did the right thing for dad, but if assisted dying had been legal would I have made a different decision on that terrible day?

Assisted dying was not legal, so it's difficult to answer that. I would certainly not have rushed to act after he asked to die, once, after a particularly bad attack of breathlessness. It's a decision that would have had to be made after long discussion, involving his doctors and palliative care specialists. It's too important a question, and so open to potential abuse, to be made by a single relative, a relative so intimately involved in the care of the patient.

14 – Decline

Life in the new flat went on as before. Dad's condition was deteriorating, but that deterioration was slow. Day to day, week to week, he appeared to be much the same. The decline showed itself in small changes, often hidden to the casual onlooker or visitor. For instance, when he showered, he sat on the shower stool and was able to take his time washing himself. It may have taken him longer than normal to shower, but he was still able to do it for himself. That is until one day, when he asked if I would help him wash his hair.

He was able to wash his body but holding his arms up to wash his hair was too much, he got out of breath in seconds.

When he asked for help I knew something dramatic had changed. Firstly, he disliked people touching his head. It all stemmed from childhood, staying at his Aunt Sue's house. He came home from school one day with a note saying that several pupils in his class had head lice and they were asking parents/guardians to treat their children for lice. Aunt Sue's idea of treatment was to grab my dad and shave his head. Her thought process was simple, no hair, no head lice. It was something that stayed with him and he hated his head being touched, even going to the barbers was an emotional roller coaster for him. So, if he was asking me to help him wash his hair, thereby touching his head, something was wrong.

Secondly, he was fiercely independent, he hated relying on other people, and he hated the thought he was becoming a burden, so if he was asking for help he must *really* need it.

Thirdly, he just didn't like asking for help, of any kind. I remember when I was a teenager, dad and I were going on a holiday with a group of friends, actually they were the darts team dad played with, we were driving to meet the group at Camber Sands. Although he was a lorry driver, and knew the motorway system extremely well, we got lost. Would dad stop and ask for help? Never! He studied maps and ploughed on. From our house to Camber Sands should have been an hour and a half drive, it took us four hours. He hated asking for help. It didn't help that from then on the darts team nicknamed him 'Pathfinder'.

When he asked me to help him wash his hair he was trying to be strong but it was obvious he was close to tears, it was a very difficult and brave thing for him to do. I knew how much it had cost him to ask, I also knew that he must have been struggling by himself for some time before he built up the emotional courage to ask. I tried to act as if it was nothing, of course I'd help him, there was no question I'd help, and in reality washing someone's hair is a simple task, but knowing what it meant to him to have to ask, I was struck virtually speechless. We both knew that this was a major sign of the erosion of his independence to come, a small sign but a significant one, nonetheless.

The first time I washed his hair was very awkward, as a very young child I remember mum washing my hair, but this was very different. The flat had two bathrooms, dad's en-suit and the main bathroom, that actually had a bath in it. The shower head came away from the wall easily, and there was more room in this bathroom, so we used this. Dad sat on his shower stool with his head over the bath and I knelt beside him with the shower head in one hand. I froze for a few seconds, I was very nervous. This felt very strange.

Dad was oddly calm, although just sitting with his head over the bath was tiring him, so I took a breath and rinsed his hair, shampooed and rinsed again… we did not repeat. The bathroom was an interior room, there were no windows, it may have been psychological, but dad found he got more breathless in such rooms. While I was drying his hair he started to get breathless, so I stopped and helped him to his bedroom, which was closer than the living room, and he sat on the bed for a few minutes.

After a few washes we perfected the process and he didn't get so out of breath. It became a rather pleasant experience, we talked to each other and it felt as if we connected on a different level.

It was around this time that I discovered the 'Carers Hub', a local organisation that offered support to carers. I contacted them and they invited me to join a group close to home, a group that met weekly for support and just a chance to chat with other people in a similar situation. I attended a few of these meetings but found that it wasn't for me, nice people though they were I just didn't feel part of the group. However, it was here that I first heard some of the stories from other carers, stories that showed just how lucky dad and I had been in our choice of general practitioner.

Our GP referred us, straight away, to St Luke's. Many of the carers at the Hub meetings were either referred too late to St Luke's or never referred at all. It was more a GP lottery than a postcode lottery. A referral opened the door to a whole range of support and getting that support early means so much for the quality of care your loved one can receive. All the preparations can be put in place early so that when needed they can be delivered almost immediately. St Luke's makes all the arrangements, without them it's a struggle to get any support at all. And as dad's rate of deterioration started to accelerate we would, I would, need all the support I could get. An example of how quickly and easily support came from St Luke's happened very soon after I started washing dad's hair.

Now that dad had asked for help once it was easier for him to ask for help, as my identity had become that of 'carer', his identity had finally changed to that of 'person needing care'. Although his next plea for assistance was quite embarrassing for the both of us.

One morning dad called me into his bedroom. He was in the en-suit, sitting on the toilet. He simply couldn't lift himself off the seat. The toilet had a handrail round it, but it was that much lower than a normal chair. He just couldn't lift himself to a standing position. I had to lift him and help him waddle to his bed. Slowly he was able to pull his trousers up and was ready to walk to the living room. The bed was positioned just right, so he was able to get to a standing position on his own and he was able to walk to the living room, with a five-minute rest stop on the hallway stool.

Over the next few days we realized that he needed help getting on and off the toilet every time. Luckily, Sue was due to visit, when she visited she usually asked how things were going and had we noticed any changes to dad's condition. Dad didn't want to say anything, even to a trusted nurse he was embarrassed to talk about such things, but I wasn't so inhibited. She suggested a commode, dad didn't like the idea at all, but she explained that the one she had in mind was more like a mini wheelchair. We could remove the bucket and dad could sit on the chair part and be wheeled to the toilet and, when he was finished, he could be wheeled back to the bed, where it would be easier to manoeuvre him onto the bed. Dad was still doubtful but I said we should try it. Sue made a phone call and the next day it arrived.

The people who delivered the commode put it together for us and even took the packaging away, why can't the people who deliver Ikea purchases do the same?

The commode stood in the corner of dad's bedroom, an ominous presence. It took a few days of me still helping dad on and off the toilet and walking him back to the bed before he agreed to try the commode. The first time he sat on it and used it dad found it wasn't as scary as his imagination had made it out to be. I simply wheeled him, backwards, over the toilet and left him to it. When he was finished he called me and I wheeled him away from the toilet and to the bed. I then helped him onto the bed and he could recover. It was much easier for both of us.

For a few weeks we carried on like this, but he was increasingly finding the walk from bedroom to living room more difficult. Getting out of bed was more of a struggle, just the process of getting to a sitting position, swinging his legs off the edge of the bed, was enough to send him into a fight for breath. It would take him about an hour to get dressed. I offered to help but he refused. It was a mix of embarrassment and pride, he had always dressed himself and he wanted to continue, no matter how long and how difficult it may be. He was very stubborn.

One day, some weeks after starting to wash his hair, dad called me into his room and told me he was going to stay in bed that day. Was there anything wrong? No, he just didn't want to get up. I handed him the tv remote and went off and got his tea. I sat with him for a while, until he needed the toilet, so he had to get out of bed. We went slowly and he didn't get too out of breath, and I left him to his own devices for a while. When he was finished I helped him back to the bed and he got back in, he still didn't want to go to the living room. He never left his bedroom again after that.

15 – Carers

The day dad decided he would stay in bed I phoned Sue to let her know. Sue had often told me to call her if anything changed, and to never worry about wasting time, it was always better to let her know. She arranged to pop in later that day. When she arrived she spent some time with dad but spent as much time with me, discussing options. She'd mentioned to dad the idea of carers coming in to help with personal hygiene matters. Dad was not comfortable with me helping him any more than I currently was but he didn't like the idea of strangers coming in to help him either.

Sue and I discussed the idea of carers and she explained that carers worked in teams, two people would visit twice a day to start with, morning and night. They could help to wash and toilet dad, they would also report back to St Luke's and our GP when needed. They would take care of the personal care issues leaving me everything else, they wouldn't 'take over' dad's care, they would supplement the care I was already providing. They would be able to do things

I might find difficult and dad might find embarrassing for his son to do. I could see the benefit of it but knew it may take some work convincing dad.

It was actually much easier to convince dad. I think he may have over heard Sue and I talking, and he had been thinking about the logistics of his care going onwards. I started the discussion by asking what he thought about Sue's suggestion of carers and, to my surprise, he said ok, let's try it. He wasn't happy about it, and to be honest I wasn't too keen, but I think we both knew it was the best thing.

My misgivings were more abstract, if professional carers came in to care for dad, what would I be? Would I still be his 'carer'? Sue said they would merely supplement what I was doing but did that mean I wasn't doing a good enough job? I had also seen numerous news stories about carers abusing their clients. The idea of that both terrified and disgusted me.

I put such thought aside and phoned Sue again, telling her that dad had agreed to having carers. She had already put things in motion and was just waiting for the go ahead from us. She would call me when everything was organised, and she could tell me when the carers would start. It was too late for them to start the following day but the day after our first pair of carers arrived at 9am.

I think one of dad's biggest worries had been the carers would be very young, and there were younger carers, but mostly they were more mature. That helped put dad at ease. They were very friendly and took everything in their stride, no matter what the issue may be, they had seen it many times before. They quickly and efficiently, but with sensitivity and kindness, washed him and helped him on and off the toilet. Their constant chatter put him at ease.

Later, when he was no longer able to get out of bed, they helped him use bed pans, and bottles, and gave him bed baths. At one point they noticed dad had a problem with dry skin, he would never have mentioned it. As soon as it was spotted they suggested I get some cream, from the doctor preferably, and they were happy to apply it. Nothing phased them and their relaxed efficiency made dad feel comfortable. Dad liked all the carers and became friends with several, actually looking forward to their visits.

My, more private and abstract, concerns were also quickly put to rest. The carers visited at 9am and 9pm, everything else was down to me. They set aside a few minutes each visit to talk with me, was there anything worrying me? or did I have any issues I'd like to discuss? They would tell me what they'd done with dad or if they'd observed anything I should know about, like the dry skin, as generally I left them alone with dad. I didn't want to intrude on dad's private time, and I didn't want the cares to feel I was keeping an eye on them.

When the end finally came, I received a lovely card and some flowers from the carers team, individually signed by all dad's carers. The comments suggested they had grown very fond of dad, as dad had grown fond of them.

16 – Life in the New Flat

Dad was now staying in bed most of the time, with just a couple of visits to the toilet, and our carefully perfected routine had to completely change. The first major change, something that really affected me, was the time dad first woke up in the morning. My bedroom was next to his. He had never liked sleeping with his bedroom door closed, something that drove me mad when I was a teenager, it had always been open, even if just a little. I had started sleeping with my door open too, so I could hear him if he called out during the night. So, I could hear him when he woke up… at between 3:30 and 4:00am.

The first thing I'd do was go in to see how he was and then went off to the kitchen. No matter how our routine changed one thing always stayed constant, three cups of tea before breakfast. Then I'd sit with him, drinking tea, and watching early morning tv news. This was during Trump's campaign for the presidency and we'd often talk, and laugh, at some of the things he'd say. We'd talk about all kinds of other things too, and the topics were very far ranging. Dad had started having some very vivid, and bizarre, dreams, and he often remembered them extremely well. He'd tell me about his dreams and we'd laugh at the often surreal situations he'd dreamt.

We also talked about the more mundane stuff of life, what to have for lunch and dinner, were there any visitors due that day, what strange things had Trump said now and what I watched on tv last night. Those very vivid dreams had a negative side, he'd started talking, and even shouting, in his sleep. Although he rarely woke himself up he always woke me up. I'd hear him talking and get up quickly and rush into his room, only to find him soundly sleeping. Some nights this happened several times, and each time I'd rush in. It also happened during the day. I'd be in the living room, doing something, and hear him talking. So, I'd go into his room only to find him asleep.

I had been an early adopter of the Apple Watch, I have to admit that I always fall for Apple's marketing. I'd pre-ordered the first Apple Watch, while still in Australia, and was one of the first people to get one. Now, I found a fantastic new use for it. I'd take my phone, put it on silent mode, and place it on his table – camera facing dad. When I heard him talking I would just lift my wrist, activate the camera remotely, and see if he was awake or asleep. It worked very well.

After his three cups of tea he would have a pre-breakfast nap. Normally this would still be before 6:00am, so I'd try to catch a few minutes sleep too, although it felt like I was always only ever half asleep. Once up I didn't go back to bed, so I'd sit in the living room, trying to nap.

At about 8:00am he'd have breakfast, he liked to have breakfast before the carers arrived at 9:00am, and his first round of medication. When the carers arrived I'd disappear into the living room, but stayed in the flat as the carers often needed to ask me something, such as where did I keep the disinfectant or clean sheets. Just before they left they'd come in to 'brief' me on how the visit went and any concerns they had. They were usually gone by 10:00am.

After they left I'd make dad a cup of tea and he'd have a couple of biscuits or a nice buttered crumpet and we'd spend a little time together before I went out to the shops, and a sneaky coffee.

That 'sneaky' coffee had become a lifeline to the 'real' world. For a few moments I was me again and not just dad's carer. It was half an hour, maybe forty-five minutes, out of the day I could just sit, eat a breakfast wrap, have a latté and try to put everything out of mind. Well, that was the theory. I'd sit, eat a breakfast wrap and drink latté, but, try as I might, I could never quite put everything out of my mind. That's where a beautiful theory breaks down.

As a carer you are constantly thinking about the person you care for, not just their condition or their symptoms but what they liked and what they were doing at that time. However, that half hour in the café was my special time and it quickly became important to me. When I finished at the café I'd go shopping. As I went shopping everyday there was never very much to get, just what was needed for that day. Dad's appetite had shrunk to that of a sparrow but he did still enjoy fish, so most days I'd go to the undercover market in Plymouth, to the fishmongers there. If they were closed I'd end up in the Marks & Spencer food hall, because they seemed to have the best selection of fish, in the shops close to the flat. Then, when fully loaded with the days catch, I'd go back to the flat.

Getting back to the flat, after shopping, was a little like getting back to a different world. In one of the Hitchhiker's Guide to the Galaxy books, 'So Long, and Thanks for All the Fish' strangely enough, Douglas Adams introduces us to a character called Wonko the Sane. Wonko had been convinced that the world was insane and the only sanity was to be found in his home, so he had signs on his front door, as you left his home you saw a sign saying "entering the asylum" and when you entered his home another sign read "leaving the asylum." When I went out of my flat, or came back to the flat, I felt a little bit like Wonko, although I didn't see the outside world as insane, not exactly. Rather, it felt like the outside world was the 'real' world and the 'world' inside the flat was a surreal, make-believe, world. Part of me could never quite accept it as real.

Back in my world of make-believe I'd make yet another cup of tea for dad and give him a couple of biscuits and get on with any housekeeping chores. I vacuumed and dusted the entire flat every day, not because I'm a clean freak (if you knew me you'd probably chuckle at the very idea) but ever since dad's COPD diagnosis I had been in a daily battle with dust. Then came the laundry.

The carers who came in twice a day seemed to generate an inordinate amount of laundry, prior to their arrival I'd maybe do a wash once a week, now it was every couple of days. I know doing the laundry is not the chore it once was. I remember how my grandmother spent an entire day hand washing the laundry, spending hours over the sink scrubbing the washing on her old washboard, and then using a hand cranked mangle to dry the washing before hanging it out to fully dry. I was lucky enough, like most people in the modern world, to have a machine that took all that drudgery out of the chore but I still had to fill the machine and then, when washed, take it out and air it before folding it and putting it away.

While I did these chores dad would half doze and half watch tv, he had become quite the daytime tv expert, 'Bargain Hunt' being one of his favourites. After the general housekeeping chores were finished it was lunchtime. Most days it was soup, dad did like his soup. Then another round of medication. After lunch dad would take his obligatory nap and I'd usually pop out for a little walk. The new flat was located in Devonport and Devonport park was just up the road and was a perfect place to have a stroll, there's even a café to spend a pleasant time sipping coffee.

When I got back to the flat dad would usually still be napping but he'd probably wake up soon after. Then it would be time for another cup of tea and a small cake or some biscuits, although he might only eat a little. We'd spend some more time together, watching tv and talking.

Dad talked about things he'd never told me before. He spent a lot of time in the past, thinking about the past at least, reliving events from his life. He'd had an interesting life in his early years and his thoughts often drifted back to those days. He talked a lot about his National Service years and his experiences in the merchant Navy. He talked about his life during the war, his various experiences of being an evacuee and the time he'd spent in London during the Blitz, playing in the rubble of bombed out buildings and searching for shrapnel.

One story he told me was when he, and a friend, had been sent to an all-girls school for a short time, they were the only two boys in a school of several hundred girls, and how terrible that had been. He talked about being a Royal Signal's dispatch rider in Egypt and one night being chased by an angry mob of locals upset by the presence of the British Army, a night he really thought he was going to die. And he talked about the friendly rivalry he had with his older brother Cliff, they liked to play one-upmanship. The best trick dad played on Cliff being when dad had won a very small amount of money on the football pools but convinced Cliff he'd actually won £25,000 (a fortune at the time).

His life had often found him in funny situations, although they may not have been that funny at the time. Now, we both laughed at some of those situations. George, his brother, once described dad as a bit of a rogue but without a malicious bone in his body. That roguish nature had seen him in trouble more than once. Like one Sunday morning in the 1950's, an incident that actually saw dad appearing in the local paper, under the headline "Was awful cheek but not theft" and in the Magistrate's Court.

On their way home, after a Saturday night out, dad and Dave, his brother-in-law, tried to start Dave's car. It wouldn't start, so they 'borrowed' an ignition coil from a neighbour's van. When an officer of Her Majesty's Constabulary asked what they were doing, dad said that "it's alright, we know the owner." In court the owner of the van said it wasn't alright, even so the magistrate declared "Most awful cheek! But there was no intention to steal."

His memories of those days were clearer, by far, than his memories of last week. And as his condition worsened, he spent more and more time thinking of, and talking about, those times and less time interested in television and current affairs.

I prepared dinner and we'd usually eat around 6 to 6:30pm and dad would just pick at his food. He had always been a fussy eater, although would strenuously deny that, but now he was hyper-fussy. Food that had always been amongst his favourites he wouldn't eat now. He'd always loved steak and kidney pudding, now he'd barely touch it. I could usually rely on him eating fish, as long as it was either pure white, as in cod, or bright yellow, for smoked haddock. Tuna or salmon he'd pick at but wouldn't enjoy.

He mentioned how much he used to like soft roe. He used to like soft herring roe, lightly fried, on toast, often as a Saturday supper treat. I remember, as a child, the house smelling of those slimy globs of goo being fried in butter while I watched Doctor Who. That smell is now inextricably linked to hiding behind the sofa watching monsters do battle with the Time Lord. I found that Waitrose stocked it, so ordered, online, some, and he woofed it up. It was a rare time when he ate like he used to. The next time I cooked some for him he barely touched it.

After dinner I'd wash up and then sit with him and we would watch a movie, we'd usually watch a western or action movie. Dad liked old movies, modern movies were difficult for him to follow, the only exceptions were modern westerns or boxing movies. These were not to my taste at all, I like old movies but am not a fan of westerns or boxing movies. However, I will treasure the time watching those dreadful movies. We'd usually get through a whole movie before the carers arrived.

The carers would then do their thing and get dad ready for the night, by around 10pm they would be gone and it would be time for dad to have a milky drink, a biscuit and his last round of medication for the day. Between 10:30 and 11pm dad would ask for his lights to be switched off and he'd settle down for the night.

After dad was settled for the night I'd go into the living room and watch something on tv, although I'd usually doze for a while. I didn't go straight to bed because I needed some time to 'unwind'. Suitably unwound I would be in bed by around midnight, ready for the whole routine to start again the next day.

17 – The End is Nigh

When we first moved into the new flat dad was still relatively mobile. He was able to get up, wash/shower, dress and walk to the living room unaided. The decline was gradual but subtlety noticeable. First, he needed my help to wash his hair. Then he needed to rest on his walk from bedroom to living room, and that rest lasted longer and longer. His recovery time, after getting to the living room, or back to his bedroom, was longer too. His breathing became more laboured and he seemed far more prone to chest infections.

After a couple of months struggling to walk from bedroom to living room dad gave in and stayed in bed all day. He still struggled to get out of bed and walk to the toilet until he wasn't able to even walk that far. Then the carers came in to help with his personal care.

By this time he was confined to bed 24 hours a day and the carers gave him bed baths, washed his hair with dry shampoo and helped him use bedpans and bottles.

Although he was confined to bed he still enjoyed watching tv and talking. The carers were a mixed bunch, but most were mature aged, one was even from South East London, near Blackheath, close to where I grew up as a child. So, dad looked forward to their visits as he had someone, other than me, to talk with.

After he battled his third chest infection his voice became very croaky. He had started watching tv less and enjoyed listening to music more, music had always been important in his life. As a lorry driver he had spent many hours on the road alone, his only companion being the radio. He liked listening to the radio, usually Radio 2. He would often sing to himself, I guess being alone in the cab of a lorry allowed him the chance to sing without the inhibition of other people being around.

Amazon had just launched its smart speaker, the Echo, in the UK, so I bought one. The idea was for dad to simply ask 'Alexa' to play his favourite music.

When the Amazon Echo arrived I excitedly set it up, and that is a tale in itself. Our broadband provider was BT and, for some reason, the Echo just wouldn't connect to BT. After a lot of tech support, from both Amazon and BT, each blaming the other, I finally got it working. I showed dad how easy it was to play his music. He liked old fashioned Country music, so I said "Alexa, play country music" and country music would start playing. Then dad tried and tried and tried again. Alexa just could not understand his voice, he couldn't get the thing to work. I think we spent half an hour trying to get Alexa to understand him, he was getting so frustrated that we had to gave up. I left the Echo in his room and used it just as a Bluetooth speaker, connected to an iPad, so dad could start and stop his music. It was just a shame he couldn't do it by voice.

After dad was confined to bed his condition seemed to stabilise for a while, or at least the deterioration was slower and less visible. He slept more and ate and drank less. It was difficult to get him to drink. His morning cups of tea were ok, that was a routine set in stone, but other times he might only have a mouthful or two of his tea and then the cup would sit on his table, ignored, getting stone cold. He always had a glass of water, mixed with cordial, near him and I tried getting him to take mouthfuls throughout the day but he only drank when I asked. He got quite upset with my constant 'nagging' and when Sue, his carers and the doctor also told him he should drink more he'd tell them he would and I'd still have to nag him. He was getting quite dehydrated. Food was not such a worry, he ate little but he was very sedentary but getting fluids into him was a problem.

The doctor, during one of his visits, had a long talk with dad, telling him just how important it was for him to drink more. Then he prescribed sachets of hydrolyte powder, just mix with water. This would help to hydrate him quicker.

He was also getting more depressed. He'd always been so active and had often said that he'd hate to end his days like this. His Aunt Sue, she who shaved his head, had been a very important person in his life. More than merely an aunt she had been more like a second mother. A larger than life character, whose life positively impacted all those she met. I wish I had known her, she died several years before I was born. During her life she had been such a fun loving and active person but at the end of her life she had spent her final weeks in bed, in agony. Dad had witnessed her decline and eventual death and had been terrified of sharing such a fate. Being confined to bed brought all that anguish and pain back to him. It seemed like he was trying to convince himself he would die the same, agonising, way.

Yes, he was confined to bed. This was because he was so very frail and his breathing made mobility difficult, or impossible. He was not, however, in much pain. We did have Oramorph in the flat but dad hardly ever needed it. In fact, one doctor suggested we use it at night as a form of sleeping potion but dad didn't like how it made him feel. He wasn't in pain, but his fear of dying with no dignity and in agony, like his Aunt Sue, was very real.

That's certainly not to say he wasn't suffering.

Here was a man who had always been proud of his independence, he had dignity, autonomy and took pride in being the one who provided for his family. He hated being helpless, as he saw it. No matter how much I said he was not, he saw himself as a burden, a burden to me and the carers. At his lowest times he'd often repeat "you wouldn't let a dog suffer like this" and "I wish you'd let me die in the caravan." There were times when he suffered physical agony. When the carers had to move him, when they washed him or changed his sheets, he would get out of breath just as if he'd done it himself. He'd struggle for breath as if he were suffocating, because he was.

Sometimes he'd try doing something, a little thing that before all this he'd never have thought about. One day the carers left his table slightly out of reach. The carers were finishing up their morning 'brief' with me in the living room when we heard him struggling for breath. He'd tried to reach his table, he'd just leant forward a little and that movement had been enough to completely drive the breath from his lungs. After that I got him a little bell, like the ones hotels sometimes have on reception, on their counter, that was in easy reach on his bedside cabinet. The only times he rang it was as a joke, but knowing it was there made him, and me, feel a little better.

As time passed his health slowly declined, he got weaker. When he spoke it was as if he were whispering, except while he was asleep. He was still able to shout out during his dreams. And as the inevitable end drew nearer he seemed to accept that end. He was resigned, no, not so much resigned as calm and accepting. He wanted to die, he was ready to die and, I think, was looking forward to death, as that would be an end to this indignity.

I would sit with him, either watching tv or listening to music, and we'd talk. He often talked about his family, family members long since gone and still living, and he often talked about what I would do when he'd gone. However, these conversations were a little disjointed as he'd frequently drift off to sleep, midsentence, waking a few minutes or an hour later.

18 – The End

In October 2016 we had a visit from dad's GP, Dr Tuckly. He spent quite some time with dad and then came into the sitting room to speak with me. He was happy with dad's medication and general care plan. A few months before he'd completed a Treatment Escalation Plan (TEP) and resuscitation decision record form with dad and now he'd just completed a new, updated, one. Dad's decision to not be resuscitated had not changed and the doctor felt it was important that I was aware of the form and what it meant, even though he'd gone through what it meant before.

Dad was very frail and both the doctor and I knew that he was very near death. When I asked the doctor if he could guess how long dad might have, he said that he doubted if dad would see his birthday. Dad was born on 11th November 1931, so his 85th birthday was very close. I felt sure that dad would still be around to celebrate his birthday, the doctor wasn't. As it turned out, I should have had a bet with the doctor. Dad was still here for his birthday.

The morning of the 11th was the same as any other Friday but as the morning approached afternoon the phone started ringing. One relative after the other rang to speak to dad, wishing him happy birthday. He had a long chat with his baby brother, George. They talked about the good old days, days so long ago that nostalgia had taken the edge off the unmitigating poverty they lived in. They talked about family members, I'd barely heard of, who had shone brightly in their lives and were now long gone. And they talked about the present, and the future. When dad finally hung up the phone there were tears on his cheeks but a smile on his face.

He and George had always had their issues. George was really dad's half-brother, they had different fathers. George was also eight years younger than dad, and when baby George had been born dad had felt some what pushed aside. He'd suppressed that feeling but it had been with him all George's life. They had always been friendly, each doing anything for the other, but there had also been an awkwardness in their relationship. During that last telephone conversation I'd watched, and heard, that awkwardness melt away.

Almost as soon as dad put the phone down it rang again. This time it was John, my brother. They spoke for a short while and the call ended. A few minutes later the phone rang again, it was David, my nephew. They spoke of a long time. When that phone call was over dad asked if I could take the phone away, he was so tired he didn't want to talk to anyone else. So, I left him to his nap and took the phone into the sitting room. While dad slept I fielded several more calls from various cousins and old family friends. Many, I think, were relieved that they didn't have to speak to the dying man. It's difficult to find what to say to someone so ill, especially over the phone.

For lunch I had got something special, a dozen oysters. When he was ready for lunch I brought them in and his eyes, which had seemed so dim lately, briefly shone. He managed to eat six of the oysters but just couldn't manage the rest. For his afternoon tea I had a small birthday cake, which he also enjoyed. When the carers came in that evening they sang happy birthday and gave him a lovely card. It may not have been like the birthdays of old, where he'd go out to the pub and celebrate with friends and family, but nonetheless it had been a good day.

During the next few days dad seemed to withdraw further into his one private world of imagination. He spent longer in the past than in the present. On the morning of the 15th November dad was pretty much the same as 'normal', he woke up at the same time, had his tea and his naps. At around 10am I had a call from the carers' manager, asking if we'd like to add a third visit, at midday. It's something we'd discussed with Sue the last time she visited, so I said yes. The manager said she'd call back, later that day, to confirm when the midday visits would start.

I then went in to see if dad wanted a drink. He did, so I made him a cup of tea and gave him a few biscuits. We sat together for a little while but when he finished his tea he asked me to turn off the tv and let him have a nap. I left him and returned to the living room, switched the tv on and started watching a movie. The living room door was open, so I could hear if he needed me. All seemed quiet, so I let him sleep. At about 1pm I went back into his bedroom, just to see if he was still sleeping. Dad was laying peacefully, with his eyes open. He looked as if he were deep in thought. I asked if he were ready for lunch, but he didn't reply. I stepped closer and asked again. Still no reply. I gently touched his arm and nothing. I realised that he'd died, alone, while I had been watching a cheap tv movie.

I'm not exactly sure when he'd died but he felt cool to the touch, so I think he'd died soon after I'd left him. He looked calm and he looked as though it had been painless.

His eyes were open and his hands were laying across his stomach. There was no tension in his hands and his face looked calm. When mum died, in Malta, dad said that she went quickly, just a quick pain and gone. He believed that because she hadn't woken him but her hands were curled up into fists, as if from a sudden jolt of pain. Dad's hands were laying open across his stomach, relaxed.

I called for an ambulance, although I knew he'd gone. The woman on the phone kept telling me to get him on the floor and to perform CPR. I knew dad didn't want to be resuscitated and I also knew that he'd been dead for a while. The ambulance arrived and confirmed he was dead. They completed some paperwork and one of the ambulance paramedics made a cup of coffee for me. They offered to stay for a while but there was nothing they could do, so I said I'd be ok. I had a lot of phone calls to make.

When they left I went back into dad's bedroom and sat next to his bed for a while, I'm not sure how long. He looked just as he had before, I kept thinking he'd turn to look at me and say something along the line of 'ha, got you!' but he didn't.

19 – The Aftermath

While I sat with dad the phone rang, it was the carers' manager. She was shocked, surprised and, I think, a little irritated, when I told her that dad had died. However, to my surprise she said that she'd let the carers know but that they would still visit that afternoon, if I wanted, so they could prepare dad and get him dressed ready for the funeral director. Normally they got to the flat at 9pm but today they'd be here at 5pm.

That phone call jolted me out of the stupor I was in, and I got on with all the preparations. I called the funeral director. I'd contacted them several weeks before and they were ready for action. The person on the phone said that they operated 24 hours a day and that when I was ready for dad to be taken to the funeral home I could just call and they'd be there, there was absolutely no rush and I could take my time. I also phoned my brother, John, and dad's brother, George. John said he'd call David, my nephew, and George, who was always one to be relied on in a crisis, said he'd phone round everyone else for me.

So, with George making the phone calls I just sat there waiting for the carers to arrive. The flat seemed so quiet and empty, I had to get out for a little, so I went for a coffee. The flat was in Devonport, very near the library. The library had, attached, a very pleasant café. I headed to the library café for a coffee and just sat there while the shock sunk in.

It's very strange, I'd been living with the expectation of his death for a long time but now that it had happened, I realised just how ill prepared I actually was. His death had been a 'thing' in our lives, a theoretical event that would manifest sometime in the future, a 'sword of Damocles' if you will. It hadn't been real. Now it had become all too real, it had happened, and I wasn't sure I could do everything that needed to be done. Wallowing in self-pity I almost forgot what time it was, 5pm was fast approaching and I had to rush back to the flat.

When the carers arrived they were fantastic. Instead of the usual two carers this visit had three. One stayed with me in the living room while the other two washed and dressed dad, ready to be picked up by the funeral director. When they had finished getting dad ready the other two came into the sitting room and we all had a cup of tea, made by one of the carers, and talked. They said how much they had enjoyed getting to know dad and that they had grown very fond of him. I'm sure they tell everyone the same thing but it helped.

I told them that I was upset that dad had died alone, while I was in the sitting room watching a b-movie on tv. One of the carers told me that a lot of terminally ill and elderly patients seemed to pick their moment to die, very often it was while they were alone. Although I felt bad about not being with him he knew how much I had done and how much I cared. I appreciated their words but it didn't make me feel any better, it's still something I deeply regret.

The carers stayed with me for about an hour and a half, longer than their usual visit, but eventually they had to go, and I was left alone again. It was no use keeping dad in the flat, the place felt so empty it was obvious he had gone. I called the funeral director and they arrived within half an hour to collect dad's body. They asked if I wanted anything left with him. On his bedside cabinet he kept a photograph of mum. I asked if that could be kept with him and they said "of course." They then brought in a casket and took him away. As he was taken it all, suddenly, felt so real, so final. While he was laying on the bed he looked as he often did, just resting. Now I couldn't fool myself. He really was gone.

The flat was emptier than ever, for so long the sound of dad's breathing had permeated the flat. It had been a sound heard all over the flat. I had often joked with him that he couldn't do anything quietly, even when he was being quiet he was noisy. I sat in the dark, not sure what I should do. Then something odd happened.

In the corner of the living room, where I was sitting, was a lamp. It was one of those lamps you just touch to turn on, touch it again and it turns off. At about 11pm, the time when dad used to ask for the lights to be turned out, the lamp decided to switch on, dim and turn off. Intellectually I know it was probably just a power spike, but it had never happened before (and never happened again). Happening as it did, on the day dad died and at the time dad used to say goodnight, I got the feeling dad had said the goodbye he never managed to say at his death. Stupid, putting such a meaning on a random power spike, but that's how my mind was working at that moment.

The next few days were busy. Dad wanted to be cremated, so there were a few things that had to be done. I spoke, over the phone, to two doctors. They asked questions about his medical history and how he died, I also spoke to dad's GP. Then I had to make an appointment to register his death and visit the funeral home. The funeral home walked me through all the options and organised everything perfectly… and relieved me of the burden of a few thousand pounds.

Dad had been an atheist all his life, before he'd even heard the word atheist. So, to honour his wishes I found a wonderful funeral celebrant, Jo, who met with me several times before the funeral to talk about dad and the family. Together we put together a beautiful eulogy, one that dad would have fully appreciated.

Jo asked if any family member wanted to speak at the funeral, George said he'd like to say a few words, so Jo incorporated George into the funeral. We picked some of dad's favourite music. Dad had been a traditional country music fan, so I picked a couple of tracks from his favourite country singers, Don Williams and Merle Haggard, and a singer from Australia that dad had loved while living there, John Williamson. Maybe not traditional funeral music but it suited dad perfectly.

Everything went smoothly, all the paperwork was completed and filed with no problems, everyone who needed to be informed was informed. The only surprise came from an unexpected source, maybe that's why it was so surprising.

On the day dad died his GP came out to certify his death, the day after the funeral I received a telephone message from the surgery inviting dad in for a check-up. I must confess that I was not amused. I called the surgery to inform them that dad couldn't come in for a check-up because he was dead. I felt like I was in Monty Python sketch. It was just a mix up, a clerical error, a computer's digital burp, but it annoyed me. The receptionist was so apologetic and sounded so, genuinely, upset about the mix up that I was sorry I had been so sarcastic and annoyed.

After the funeral, and after all the bustle and fuss had died down, life had to go on. Dad died on the 15th of November, and Christmas was looming. I knew that I didn't want to be in the flat over Christmas. I'd never liked being at home over Christmas, well, not since I was a child. I usually went away somewhere, so I decided to find somewhere I'd never been before and go away for Christmas and New Year. After a little while on the internet, and making a few phone calls, I was booked into a lovely hotel in Aberdeen, Scotland.

20 – Life after Death

On a bitterly cold December day, the 20th to be exact, I boarded an early morning train in Plymouth and after over eleven hours, and a few train changes, I arrived in Aberdeen. It was a short taxi ride from the station to the hotel. After that journey I wished I'd chosen to spend Christmas in Spain, the journey would have been quicker and it might have been a lot warmer.

The hotel was beautiful, the room was comfortable and had everything you could possibly need. It was a pleasant, and short, walk into the heart of the city, which was beautiful. The Christmas market, in the city centre, was a true Christmas wonderland, I even found a stall that catered to my desire for bratwurst.

As I normally do, I found a comfortable routine. I was still rising early, about 6am, so I was normally one of the first guests in the dining room for breakfast, which would be long and hearty. Then I'd return to my room, read the newspaper and have a coffee, and venture out at about 10am. I'd walk into the city centre, visit a museum, see a few places of interest or do some shopping and then find a comfortable café to have a few coffees and read for a while. Have lunch and another stroll through the city before going back to the hotel for a nap and, later, dinner, usually in the hotel restaurant, which served delicious local food.

Christmas Day lunch was a very grand affair, it was just what you'd want from a Scottish Christmas: roaring logs fire, pipers piping, plates laden with food and huge amounts of Scottish cheer, in the form of a thousand types of whiskey. New Year was the same, only louder with more dancing.

On January 4th I checked out of the hotel and boarded the train bound for sassanak land, and another eleven-hour journey. After spending Christmas and New Year in Scotland, I was glad I'd chosen Aberdeen over Spain, I'd even seen snow on Boxing Day.

Getting back to the flat was a real coming back down to earth, back to the mundane world. I wasn't sure what I was going to do or even who I was now. Who are you when your identity is taken away? My identity was 'carer', if I had no one to care for, who was I? I didn't feel ready to go back to teaching and I wasn't ready to go back to Australia. So, I bought a piano and embarked to a long-held wish to learn to play a musical instrument.

The wish to learn to play an instrument started at secondary school, when I was 11 years old. When I started secondary school we went through an induction, taking introduction classes in everything, even if you had no intention of picking those subjects later on. So, we all studied music. The lessons were pretty basic, we learnt to play a hugely simplified version of Clare de Lune on the recorder, but the teacher said anyone who wanted to learn an instrument should meet him in the music room at lunchtime. I was there. I had always wanted to play the trumpet, so I signed up for music lessons.

At the first afterschool lesson, Mr Trubman, took one look at me and said the tuba would suit me better. So, I was lent a tuba, given a book and shown how to blow. I could take the tuba home to practice, so of course I did. Later that evening, when dad got home from work, I was practicing in the living room. He heard me and suggested the best place to practice might be the garden. I went out and sat on the steps in the garden, my back to the house, Oom Pah Pahing to my hearts content when, suddenly, the clear ringing from the instrument went glug glug glug. Dad had crept up behind me and poured a bottle of water down my tuba, in an attempt to save the neighbourhood from the dreadful sound. The neighbours may have thanked him but I didn't. That was the end of my music ambitions, and it took many years before I could see the funny side of the incident.

Later I became part of a music group at St Luke's Hospice. The group was set up by Jutta, the director of their Social Care team, to help people who had suffered a bereavement. There's about eight of us in the group and we sing, play instruments and generally make a lot of noise, but it's all great fun. The group is so much more than just music, it's become a group of friends, we even meet up for lunch and a chat when the music part of the group in on hiatus. It's more of a support group that uses music as a form of social grease, making it easier to talk and share stories. We've laughed and cried together.

21 – A Final Word

Talking to people who have lost a loved one, or are about to experience such a loss, one thing has been made clear, everyone experiences grief differently. Some fall apart and find it difficult to cope, others are stoic, and pull themselves together and get on with life, and everything in between. And that's as it should be, in life everyone is unique so why would death be any different?

The death of a loved one can be sudden, and be completely unexpected, or it can be a long drawn out process with the death totally expected. It doesn't matter how you lose someone, you still feel a bit like a grape hit by a freight train. When my mum died it was a total surprise. Just the day before her death, she had told us she'd never felt better, and then she died and that freight train struck. When my dad died it was expected, we'd been living with his impending death for over a year, yet when I found him, on his bed, dead that same freight train still struck.

The only difference between the two deaths was that when my mum died I had a network of support around me, I remember going to dinner the night mum died. All five of us, dad, me, John, Kath and Jane, walked down the street, hand in hand, as though it were us against the world. In that moment I had never felt so sad yet so loved. I belonged to a group who shared my grief and we all supported each other through it.

However, when dad died I was alone. My friends were all half-way around the world and my family were scattered around the country. If it hadn't been for the carers on the day, I'd have been totally alone, although the day after I had no one. Since moving back to the UK I had been dad's carer. My life had been completely dominated by that role, that identity. I hadn't had time, or the will, to make friends.

After dad died I was lucky, I found support from St Luke's, in the form of Jutta, their director of social care, who gave me time to talk about my grief and then, later, gave me a group to belong to. Now, I help other people find that support, and find someone to talk about their grief to. Plymouth has become a Compassionate City and part of that is opening Compassionate Cafés, places people can go, have a coffee, and chat to someone about anything they need to.

I still miss dad, he had been such a positive figure in my life, and a real character. But now, the loss is not a raw feeling. It's a mellow sense of sadness but I can remember the happy times. Now, when I think of my dad I smile far more than I want to cry.

www.ingramcontent.com/pod-product-compliance
Lightning Source LLC
Chambersburg PA
CBHW061651040426
42446CB00010B/1690